HISTORY OF
COLORADO'S WOMEN
FOR YOUNG PEOPLE

Written and Illustrated by
Vivian Sheldon Epstein

Copyright © 1998 by Vivian Sheldon Epstein
All rights reserved. Printed in U.S.A.
ISBN 1-891424-01-7
No part of this book may be used or reproduced in any manner
whatsoever without written permission except in the case of brief quotations.
For information address: VSE Pubisher, 212 South Dexter Street,
Denver, Colorado 80246

ACKNOWLEDGEMENTS

I am appreciative of the many authors who wrote books about Colorado and the numerous articles written about women in magazines and newspapers, primarily the *Rocky Mountain News* and *The Denver Post*. I am thankful to the librarians and teachers who for twenty years have suggested that I write this book. The resource material and the helpful librarians of the reference and Western History Department of the Denver Public Library and the library of the Colorado Historical Society have been invaluable.

I always feel extremely lucky to have a thoughtful, sensitive, and loving husband, **Ted Epstein, Jr.**, who has offered excellent suggestions and constant encouragment to me as an author and in all my life endeavors.

I am indebted to the following people who gave me their time, expertise, and suggestions:

Brenda Sheldon, my sister-in-law, who has given me her excellent editorial suggestions graciously, with careful attention to detail

Elizabeth Epstein, my daughter, computer expert and Denver attorney, who is a wonderful example of a self-confident and self-actualized woman

Norman Sheldon, my multi-talented brother, who has photographed the pages of my books for my lectures, made editorial suggestions, and brought me into the 20th century world of computers and technology

Walter Mielziner, thorough proof reader and aerospace engineer

Eleanor Gehres, Manager Western History/General Department, Denver Public Library

Pam Marioneaux, Manager Children's Library, Denver Public Library

Joanne Dodds, Assistant Director of the Pueblo Library District

Keller Hayes, president Colorado Women's Chamber of Commerce

Madeline A. Collison, president of the Colorado Women's Bar Association and attorney at law with Feiger & Collison, P.C., Denver

Chris Petteys, author of *Dictionary of Women Artists, an international dictionary of women artists born before 1900*

Elizabeth Schlosser, private art dealer specializing in Colorado art, past executive director of Historic Denver, Inc. and of Historic Paramount Foundation and author of *Modern Art in Denver, 1919-1960* and *Modern Sculptures in Denver, 1919-1960*

Vicki Cowart, State Geologist and Director of the Colorado Geological Survey

Jane Withers, founder and first president of the Women's Chamber of Commerce and owner of Hub Cap Annie's

Patricia Gabow, M.D., CEO and Medical Director of Denver Health

Sherri Vasquez, president of the Colorado Hispanic Media Association and feature writer for the *Rocky Mountain News*

Wallace Yvonne McNair, Administrator of the Black American West Museum & Heritage Center

Marie Adams, Curatorial Assistant, Department of Painting and Sculpture, Denver Art Museum

Joan Birkland, Executive Director of Sports Women of Colorado

Charles Hohnstein, president of Quality Press, printer of this book, whose company's name represents his high standards

INTRODUCTION

Courage and Creativity
Both women and men gave their talents and abilities to make the Colorado we know today. History books are filled with the contributions men have made. Very few books discuss women's work. The traditional role of women has been to care for the family and home. This book emphasizes women's work in a variety of careers. Many women had the courage and creativity to overcome huge obstacles in their paths. Readers of this book should be inspired by these life stories to fully use their own talents.

Selection of Women for this Book
For most careers, women need a good education. Sometimes they were excluded from a career; sometimes they had to work several years to pay for their additional education. Only a few careers and a few women, all with ties to Colorado, are discussed in this book. The author selected women who were firsts in a field, whose accomplishments helped others in a positive way, who were part of the exciting stories of Colorado and whose names appeared often in books, newspapers and magazine articles. A few are highlighted at the front of the book. Many are listed at the end. The names and contributions of hundreds of thousands of women and their work in and out of the home remain unlisted due to space limitations.

Overview
This book is intended to be an overview of what some Colorado women have accomplished. One cannot reduce a person's life to fifteen typed lines. However, after much reading about each individual, the author tried to state simply the essence or most important parts of what each woman has done. Many of the women in the book received awards and honors, and were inducted into various halls of fame. Only in a few instances are these honors mentioned due to space limitations. It is hoped that the reader will want to delve further into the lives of some of the women presented through additional reading and research.

Courage and Determination
The book begins with those who were first here, the Native Americans, descended from ancient people. Other women traveled many miles, arriving in Colorado. The many states and some countries from which they came are listed after each woman's name. They left the safety and comfort of their homes to make a new and often better life. These women had courage and determination, both as early pioneers and as pioneers who entered traditional male careers. They are role models who paved the way.

Omissions
The author apologizes for errors and omissions. Some omissions of people, dates, and facts are due to the fact that records were not kept. Most omissions are due to lack of space in this book. Almost every living woman selected for this book was contacted by the author for accuracy. Many statements from other sources were questioned and checked. The author welcomes the reader to write regarding corrections and additions and she may be able to include new information in future printings.

Each of us must use our talents for our own fulfillment and to help make Colorado and our world a better place.

I love our beautiful state of Colorado and am always thankful to be living here. My dear parents, Herman and Hilde Sheldon, made a wonderful choice in selecting Colorado for our home.

It was a great joy for me to research, write and illustrate this book. I was learning about, speaking with, and meeting the dynamic women of Colorado.

Vivian Sheldon Epstein

TABLE OF CONTENTS

Introduction............................	1, 2, 4, 5
Chipeta...................................	6
Helen Hunt Jackson.................	7
Clara Brown............................	8
Frances Wisebart Jacobs..........	9
Augusta Pierce Tabor...............	10
Baby Doe Tabor......................	11
Margaret (Maggie) Brown........	12
Florence Sabin........................	13
Emily Griffith..........................	14
Josephine Roche.....................	15
Frances (Pinky) Wayne............	16
Mary Elitch Long....................	17
Justina Ford............................	18
Achieving The Right To Vote...	19
Ruth Murray Underhill.............	20
Helen G. Bonfils.....................	21
Muriel Sibell Wolle.................	22
Antonia Brico.........................	23
Mildred (Babe) Didrikson Zaharias..	24
Ruth Mosko Handler...............	25
Dana H. Crawford..................	26
Patricia Schroeder...................	27
Joyce Meskis..........................	28
Judith Albino.........................	29
Cleo Parker Robinson..............	30
Dolores S. Atencio..................	31
Linda Alvarado.......................	32
Amy Van Dyken......................	33.

Lists of Achievements

The Arts...Actor, Television, Director.....	34
Anthropologists, Architects.....................	35
Artists...Painters, Sculptors.....................	35, 36
Banking and Business............................	37, 38
Directors and Managers.........................	38, 39
Education...	39, 40
Firefighters...	40
Judicial and Legal.................................	41
Music..	42
Political and Government.....................	42, 43, 44, 45
Publishers, Writers, Journalists..............	45, 46, 47
Science: Medicine...............................	47, 48
Science: Geology, Engineering.............	48
Sports..	49
Volunteer Activists................................	50, 51, 52
Bibliography...........................	55, 56

For thousands of years, people have lived in Colorado. Some left only a trace of their existence: part of a woven basket or clay pot, remains of their homes carved into mountain cliffs. Some came to explore Colorado or trade in furs and left us with words from their Spanish and French languages. Some people like Native Americans who cherish our earth, left us with their values.

Native American women and men each did work to help their tribe. Women cared for the home, often setting up and taking down their shelter of the tepee. They cared for the children, gathered and prepared food, made clothing out of animal skins, wove baskets and cloth.

When gold was discovered in Colorado in 1858, men came seeking riches, adventure, and freedom. Some of the gold miners brought their wives and families; some women came alone.

They traveled in covered wagons through blizzards, floods, and windstorms. Some women who came to Colorado left beautiful homes with fine furniture and lace curtains. Their first Colorado home on a site without trees had one small, dark, damp room dug into the side of a hill. Some other homes were made of sod by cutting bricks of grass and soil. Home sites with many trees provided logs, and one-room cabins were built with floors made of dirt.

The pioneer women cared for their children, prepared meals, baked bread, wove cloth and sewed clothing, planted vegetables and grains, found plants and herbs to cure sickness, made soap and candles out of animal fat, protected the family against attacking animals and people, and coped with loneliness.

Both the Native American women and the pioneer women had great inner strength and courage.

For over 10,000 years, Native Americans lived on the land we now call Colorado. Some of the tribes were the Arapaho, Cheyenne, Kiowa, Pawnee and Ute. The United States government forcibly moved the Native Americans from their land and stopped them from living the ways of their ancestors.

CHIPETA   (1843-1924   Colorado, Utah)

Chipeta, loved and respected wife of the Ute Chief Ouray, helped Colorado pioneers through her brave peace efforts.

People of the Ute tribe found a young Kiowa Apache girl and raised her, naming her Chipeta, which means White Singing Bird. At age sixteen, Chipeta married Ouray, who became Chief of the Utes. In addition to the traditional work performed by women in the tribe, Chipeta also was one of the few women allowed to hunt. Both Chipeta and Chief Ouray worked for peace between the Utes and the white people. Chipeta always joined Chief Ouray when he was invited to Washington, D.C. to sign peace treaties. Chipeta's bravery was often seen. When knowing that her white neighbors were going to be killed, she swam through the dangerous currents of the Gunnison River, arriving in time to warn the settlers. In 1879 when Chief Ouray was away, twenty-five Utes captured white women and children and killed the U.S. government's representative, Nathan Meeker. Alone, Chipeta rode 100 miles on ponies to the mountains to alert her husband so he could help regain peace. After Ouray's death, the U.S. government cruelly sold all of Chipeta's possessions and moved her and the entire tribe to a reservation in Utah. For the next forty-four years, Chipeta lived in great poverty. After her death, people realized the great injustice done to her. The secretly-buried remains of Chipeta and Chief Ouray were brought back to Montrose, Colorado, today resting in Ouray Memorial Park.

HELEN HUNT JACKSON (c.1830-1885 Massachusetts, Colorado, California)

Through her book, *Ramona*, author, Helen Hunt Jackson, made people aware of the terrible treatment of Native Americans.

By the time she was fifteen years old, both of Helen's parents had died. She then lived with relatives and friends and married West Point graduate, Captain Edward Hunt, when she was twenty-one. Her happiness and security were again taken from her with three more tragic deaths: her infant son died, her husband was killed in an accident, and her only other child died of illness. To help heal her great sadness, Helen began to write poems about grief, death and love. To support herself financially, she sent her writings to popular magazines and immediately became one of the most successful women writers in America. She also wrote children's stories, travel articles and short novels. Because of lung problems in her early forties, Helen moved to Colorado Springs. She lived in a boarding house, where she met and married another boarder, William S. Jackson, who was one of the founders of Colorado Springs. After learning of the terrible treatment of Native Americans by the U.S. government, Helen researched and wrote *A Century of Dishonor*. She placed a copy on the desk of every senator in Congress. When her work was ignored, Helen used the same facts in fiction form, writing the book, *Ramona*, which was widely read. Helen Hunt Jackson made the public and Congress aware of the injustice and some laws were passed protecting Native Americans.

CLARA BROWN   (1803-1885 Virginia, Kentucky, Missouri, Kansas, Colorado)

Clara Brown, a freed slave, cared for others and shared her wealth. At her own expense, she brought sixteen African-American freed slaves from Kentucky to Colorado, paying for their food, clothing, and transportation.

Clara was born a slave, and married at age eighteen. Seventeen years later, her entire family of husband and children were taken from her. Her master had died and her loved ones were all sold to different owners. Clara worked as a slave for twenty more years, but when this master died, Clara purchased her freedom with money both she and the master's helpful daughters had saved. At age fifty-five, Clara wanted to improve her life by going to Colorado, where many people were seeking gold. In exchange for cooking and doing laundry, she was taken on the eight to ten week journey by covered wagon from Kentucky to Colorado in 1859. She followed the prospectors from Denver to Central City, setting up her laundry of stoves and tubs in the mining camp, charging fifty cents per shirt. "Aunt" Clara Brown nursed the miners. Her home became a hospital, hotel and even a place for church services. Having saved ten thousand dollars and making shrewd land investments, independent Clara now traveled to Virginia and Kentucky to search for her daughter, the only living member of her family. Clara had not seen her for forty-four years! Unable to find her, Clara Brown generously used her hard earned money to bring sixteen freed slaves with her to Colorado to begin a better life. Almost eighty, she finally was reunited with her daughter and honored with membership into The Society of Colorado Pioneers.

FRANCES WISEBART JACOBS   (1843-1892 Kentucky, Colorado)

Frances Wisebart Jacobs has been the only woman selected for a stained glass portrait in the dome of Colorado's State Capitol. She began many charity organizations, including the forerunner of the Mile High United Way.

As a young girl, Frances was a tomboy. This trait helped her in the rugged frontier life she faced after marriage to Abraham Jacobs, owner of a Central City clothing store. Some of the people who had come to Colorado in search of gold and had not found it had no money left for food. Frances noticed and because her Jewish religion taught her to be kind to strangers, she used her own money to help poor people. She knew that charity should come from everyone and should be given to anyone who needed it. The family moved to Denver and she continued her good deeds. Frances spoke convincingly to religious and social leaders and, with their support, helped start the first free kindergarten in Denver, found homes and good employment for homeless women, collected clothing for the poor, and established homes for the sick and elderly. She began a free hospital for people unable to pay. This was named the Frances Jacobs Hospital and is today The National Jewish Medical and Research Center. Frances wanted all the charities to work together in one organization, each contributing money. The Charity Organization Society was formed. Today this is Denver's Mile High United Way. With her kind heart and great organizing skills, Frances Wisebart Jacobs laid the foundations for the charity work of Colorado.

AUGUSTA PIERCE TABOR (1833-1895 Maine, Kansas, Colorado)

Augusta Tabor's courage, hard work, ability to save money, and loyalty to her husband helped lay the foundation for his great wealth. After a twenty-five year marriage, she was divorced by her husband, who married Baby Doe.

Augusta, cousin of U.S. President, Franklin Pierce, was named for the capital of her native state, Maine. She fell in love with Horace Tabor who worked for her father as a stone cutter. Ambitious Horace bought land to farm in Kansas, returning to marry Augusta. With two other men for protection, Augusta and Horace traveled to Kansas by oxen in rain and tremendous windstorms. Coming from a lovely New England home, she was shocked at the tiny windowless one-room cabin Horace had already built for her in Kansas. When the crops they planted died without rain, Horace decided to seek gold in Colorado. Traveling from Denver to the Leadville, Colorado area, took three difficult months. To earn money, Augusta shared their one-room cabin with boarders. She made and sold baked goods and dinners, weighed prospectors' gold dust, was appointed town Post Mistress and began a store. She and son Maxcy worked long hours; the store thrived. Horace's mines yielded enormous amounts of gold and silver making them very wealthy. Augusta disapproved of the great amount of money Horace was spending. Horace wanted a divorce so he could marry Baby Doe; Augusta unhappily agreed. Eventually, Horace lost all his money. Augusta, by wise investing and saving, had over one million dollars. She offered to help Horace; he refused the help.

BABY DOE TABOR   (1854-1935 Wisconsin, Colorado)

Baby Doe, as the second wife of multi-millionaire and silver king Horace Tabor, knew a life of incredible wealth. When silver lost its value, Horace went bankrupt. Baby Doe lived her last thirty-five years in great poverty in a one-room cabin, where she was found frozen to death.

Elizabeth McCourt, nicknamed Baby by her brother when she was young, was always thought to be a great beauty. She married Harvey Doe and moved with him to Colorado to seek gold. Bored as a homemaker, she decided to work with her husband in their mine. People thought this was not proper work for a woman. Because the mine did not produce any gold, Harvey became discouraged, drank too much alcohol, and was soon divorced by Baby Doe. Horace Tabor was Lieutenant Governor of Colorado and a multi-millionaire because of the silver his mines were producing. He met and fell in love with Baby Doe. Both had a zest for life, loved material possessions, and were interested in mining. Horace divorced Augusta Tabor, married Baby Doe, and lived lavishly. Colorado women would not come to the wedding nor would they ever accept Baby Doe, as their loyalty was to Augusta. Horace and Baby Doe had two daughters; both eventually rejected their mother. Silver had lost its value and Horace had lost all his money, but Baby Doe remained with him. Horace had thought silver would rise in value. He was wrong, but Baby Doe loved and believed him. After Horace died, she lived alone for thirty-five years in a small cabin near their Matchless Mine in Leadville, Colorado. Baby Doe Tabor had sold all her jewels, had ragged clothing, little food, and died, frozen to death.

MARGARET (MAGGIE) BROWN (1867-1932 Missouri, Colorado)

Maggie Brown was called "The Unsinkable Molly Brown" because she survived the sinking of the *Titanic* and managed to stay on top of the Denver social scene.

Lured by the excitement of finding gold, Margaret, called Maggie, followed her half-sister to Leadville, Colorado. A mining foreman, thirty-one year old J.J. Brown, fell in love and married nineteen year old Maggie. They had two children. J.J. Brown had invested in the Ibex Mining Company. Suddenly, huge quantities of the purest gold and copper were found in one of the company's mines, The Little Jonny. J.J. and Maggie became very rich. The family moved to Denver, bought an expensive home, and gave lavish parties. Some of Denver's "elite" society rejected Maggie. Perhaps Maggie reminded them of their own rise from poverty to riches. Maggie, wanting to become a social leader, generously donated to charity and improved her education by studying literature and languages. Her husband, J.J. was uncomfortable with this new way of life. They agreed to separate, ending twenty-three years of marriage. Vacationing in Europe, Maggie rushed home to be with her ill grandson. She sailed home on the ship, the *Titanic*, which struck an iceberg in the Atlantic Ocean and sank. Maggie rowed one of the lifeboats, saving many passengers. She became a national celebrity, "The Unsinkable Mrs. Brown." Her life story inspired a theatrical play and movie. Historic Denver Inc. was created to save her home, The Molly Brown House, located at 1340 Pennsylvania.

FLORENCE SABIN   (1871-1953   Colorado, Maryland, New York, Colorado)

Each state in the U.S. has selected two citizens who best represent their state, and a statue of each is in Washington, D.C., Statuary Hall in the Capitol. Hardly any are women. Colorado selected Dr. Florence Sabin.

One of the greatest women research scientists, Florence Sabin had three careers: teaching future doctors at Johns Hopkins University, researching at the Rockefeller Institute for Medical Research, and heading and reforming the Colorado Health Department.

Sadly, on Florence Sabin's seventh birthday, her mother died. When her father could no longer give her a home, she and her sister lived in boarding schools and with relatives. Florence wanted to become a doctor, a career her father had wanted for himself but had never realized. She taught school for three years to pay for her medical school training. While still a medical student, brilliant Florence made discoveries about the human lymph system, helping doctors better understand the body. Florence achieved many "firsts" for a woman: first woman professor at Johns Hopkins Medical School and researcher at the Rockefeller Institute; first woman elected president of the American Association of Anatomists; and first woman awarded membership in the National Academy of Sciences. She retired to her home state of Colorado, but not to rest. From the age of seventy-three to eighty, Florence was challenged by four Colorado governors to improve the health of Colorado's people. Florence taught the public and law makers about ways to prevent disease, and the "Sabin Health Bills" became law. Rats in cities were gone, water and milk were purified, restaurants had rules of cleanliness, and better medical services were provided. Dr. Florence Sabin had re-organized and greatly improved the Health Departments of both Denver and Colorado.

EMILY GRIFFITH (1880-1947 Ohio, Nebraska, Colorado)

Emily Griffith created Opportunity School, the world's first school where adults and young people could learn whatever they wanted and needed to expand their opportunities in life.

At age fourteen, Emily helped earn money for her family by becoming a school teacher. She taught in a sod schoolhouse and lived in the homes of her students, some of whom were older than she. To improve their finances, her father moved his frail wife and four children to Denver in 1895. Emily continued teaching. For the next thirty years, Emily either taught or visited Colorado schools through her job as Deputy State Superintendent of Schools. She became involved in the lives of students and their families. Many were poor and Emily knew more education would help them. Emily wanted to create a school to give people more opportunities. It should be open day and night, for both adults and young people, with a sign above the school entrance stating *For All Who Wish To Learn*. Emily Griffith finally convinced the Denver School Board and Opportunity School opened in 1916 at 13th and Welton Street in Denver. Emily, as principal and teacher, encouraged thousands to improve their lives through learning what they wanted and needed, such as welding, car repair, or floral arranging. U.S. and world educators came to learn about this remarkable school. Awards and honors were given to Emily. One year after her retirement, the school was renamed The Emily Griffith Opportunity School.

JOSEPHINE ROCHE (1886-1976 Nebraska, Colorado)

Josephine Roche was a social crusader and leader in the field of industrial relations. Through her careers in business and politics and with her great compassion for others, she helped reform child labor laws and the rights of women in the workplace. She spoke and created positive changes for people who could not help themselves.

Josephine graduated from Vassar College and Columbia University. Her degree in social work introduced her to ideas which strengthened her social conscience. Joining her family in Denver, she was appointed Denver's first woman police officer. Angry at the terrible living conditions of poor women and children, she became their protector, speaking for them. She fought for child labor laws and fearlessly attacked businesses and politicians who caused misery for children and women in the workplace. When her father died, she became the head of his Denver business, the Rocky Mountain Fuel Company. Wanting to help her employees, she shocked other mining company owners by inviting the unions into her company. She then raised the wages of the miners working for her to the highest in the coal industry. The Depression caused her business to fail. Wanting to help all Coloradans, she ran to be a candidate for governor of Colorado, but lost. Her reputation as a humanitarian who cared greatly about people and as an outstanding employer was noticed by the President of the United States, Franklin Roosevelt. He appointed her Assistant Secretary of Labor in 1934. Josephine Roche became the second woman in the United States to hold a high office in the federal government. She continued to act on her ideals of treating all people with dignity.

FRANCES (PINKY) WAYNE (1870-1951 Indiana, Washington, D.C., Colorado)

Newspaper journalist Frances Wayne, cared deeply about many causes. For forty years, her news stories and opinions influenced people and created positive change.

Frances was called Pinky because of her red hair. Pinky gained her interest in community affairs from her publically-active parents. Her father, James Belford, was the first man elected to the U.S. House of Representatives from Colorado. Her mother was the first woman member of the State Board of Charities and was trustee of two Colorado colleges. When Pinky began writing for the *Rocky Mountain News* in 1906, she covered society events and soon became their drama and music critic. She was hired by *The Denver Post*, where she wrote about issues usually covered by men: murders, political campaigns, and coal miners strikes. Pinky was not afraid to write about controversial subjects such as children's rights, women's rights and birth control. Emily Griffith's wonderful idea of creating an opportunity school for adult education might have remained just a dream; Pinky Wayne's articles created the necessary public support. Pinky's vivid stories about the needs of emotionally ill people helped create funding for the state hospital in Pueblo. After almost forty years with *The Denver Post,* she was fired at age seventy-six. She moved to her childhood home in Central City, Colorado, becoming editor of the third oldest Colorado newspaper. Frances Wayne's newspaper crusades created positive changes for the people of Colorado.

MARY ELITCH LONG   (1850-1936 Pennsylvania, California, Colorado)

Mary Elitch Long was the co-founder and developer of Elitch Gardens Amusement Park and a successful business woman. She created the first theatrical summer stock company in the United States.

Mary Elizabeth Hauck, born in Philadelphia, moved to California with her parents in early childhood. Her father's business of ranching and farming planted seeds of interest in Mary's life. At age sixteen, she married John Elitch, Jr., an actor and athlete. John's dream of many years was to own a park where rare animals and birds could be seen and enjoyed by the public. Mary loved and encouraged this idea. Five years after their 1882 arrival in Denver, they purchased sixteen acres filled with trees in Highlands, which is today part of Denver. Rare animals were purchased. The smallest locomotive and cars in the world were built for them, traveling on tracks laid throughout the park. Despite a rainy May 1890 opening day, the crowds arrived. Less than a year later, John died. Mary Elitch courageously chose to continue her husband's vision and became the sole manager of Elitch Gardens and the only woman in the world to run an amusement park. Even after her second marriage to Thomas Long, she continued as manager until 1916. She brought theatre with well-known actors, orchestra and band concerts and maintained a thriving animal zoo. She began a weekly Childrens' Day program with classes in nature study and drama. Mary Elitch gave us beauty and culture through her gardens, music, and summer theatre.

JUSTINA FORD (1871-1952 Illinois, Alabama, Missouri, Colorado)

Justina Ford, first African-American woman doctor in Colorado, set an example of dedication and compassionate care. Her office/home is now the location of The Black American West Museum & Heritage Center. In 1984, the house was placed on the National Register of Historic Landmarks.

Justina was one of seven children. Inspired by her mother's medical career as a nurse, her favorite childhood game was to play hospital; Justina insisted on being the doctor. Acting on this dream, she received her medical degree in 1899. Three years later she arrived in Denver as the first black woman doctor. Denver General Hospital reflected the terrible prejudices of society: neither black patients nor black doctors were allowed. Justina then practiced at home, using the main floor as her medical offices and living on the upper floor. She vowed to help all people, ignoring the color of their skin. Her patients were black and white, American Indian, Chinese, Japanese, Spanish and Greek. Dr. Ford also made many home visits, where she helped deliver 7,000 babies during her fifty-year career. She arrived in the homes by street car or taxi. The taxi company never charged her for the fare, knowing that Dr. Justina Ford usually did not charge the families she helped. They were often too poor to pay, but might give Justina eggs or a chicken in exchange. Despite receiving little money, Dr. Ford gave her savings to young people for their own education. After her death, Dr. Justina Ford's home was saved from destruction and is a place of continuing education as The Black American West Museum & Heritage Center.

The women so far discussed in this book had great personal strengths, but publicly had no voice. United States law did not allow women to vote! However, each state was allowed to make its own decision.

ON NOVEMBER 7, 1893, COLORADO BECAME THE SECOND STATE IN THE UNITED STATES TO GRANT WOMEN THE RIGHT TO VOTE.

Most men thought women should concentrate on being mothers and homemakers. Influenced by some women in England who knew voting was their right, Elizabeth Cady Stanton and Lucretia Mott organized the first Women's Rights Convention held at Seneca Falls, New York, in 1848. Finally in 1920, all women in the United States were granted the right to vote by the 19th Amendment to the U.S. Constitution.

For twenty-seven years, the battle to win the right to vote for Colorado's women was fought by both women and men. Some newspaper editors and governors tried to change public opinion. National leaders came to Colorado to help convince the male voters to give women the right to vote. Petitions were signed. At the same time, Colorado was about to become a state. In 1877, the vote was NO! The many women and men who had worked so hard were very discouraged. Sixteen years passed. A few talented women who wrote for newspapers created renewed interest in the vote for women. A bill was introduced, once again, asking voters to grant women the right to vote. **SUCCESS**! The vote was **YES**. When Governor Waite signed the bill into law on November 7, 1893, women of Colorado became full citizens.

RUTH MURRAY UNDERHILL (1884-1984 New York, Massachusetts, Italy, Washington, D.C., Colorado)

Dr. Ruth Murray Underhill helped Arizona's Papago Indian people regain a pride in their heritage through her study of their culture. She shared her knowledge about other cultures in her twenty-six books and pamphlets and as a University of Denver anthropology professor.

After graduating Vassar College, Ruth had several jobs doing social work. She helped protect children. She saw many unhapppy people in her work and wanted to understand more about human behavior. After age forty, Ruth returned to school, earning a Ph.D. in anthropology from Columbia University. Anthropology is the study of people in different cultures. Her teacher, Dr. Franz Boaz, suggested Ruth study the culture of the Papago Indians of Arizona. Ruth spent three summers living in a tent and learning about the Papago people. The Papago Indians did not write words; instead they had an oral tradition. Dr. Ruth Underhill was the first person to put their language into words, translated them into English, and collected all their songs, poems and legends. Ruth asked many questions, carefully watched actions and body language and then wrote what she had observed. For example, a Papago does not say thank you for a gift, but responds with good deeds. Dr. Underhill worked for the U.S. Bureau of Indian Affairs for thirteen years, visiting tribes all over the country. She recorded their legends and values, which became books used in Indian schools. From 1947 to 1961, Dr. Ruth Underhill taught anthropology at the University of Denver. She worked as an anthropologist until the end of her long life, having written twenty-six books and pamplets.

HELEN G. BONFILS (1889-1972 New York, Colorado)

Helen G. Bonfils enriched the lives of the people of Denver through her generous charitable contributions to the theatre, arts, public and private charities, hospitals, schools, and churches. The Helen G. Bonfils Foundation helped create The Denver Center for the Performing Arts.

Helen gained an interest in business from her father and a love of theatre from her mother. As daughter of Frederick Bonfils, the co-founder of *The Denver Post* newspaper, Helen grew up hearing about the world of business, publishing and real estate. She often went with her mother and grandmother to afternoon theatre productions. Helen began to act in plays, and while performing at the Elitch Theatre, met and married the director, George Somnes when she was forty-six years old. They kept homes in Denver and New York City and together produced several Broadway plays and ran the Elitch Theatre. After the death of her father in 1933, Helen became secretary-treasurer of *The Denver Post*, rising to president and chairman of the board in 1966. Helen was able to stop a takeover attempt of the newspaper to outside interests and made it possible for the employees of *The Denver Post* to buy and eventually own the newspaper. She wanted to continue the charitable work her parents had begun and created the Belle Bonfils Memorial Blood Bank in memory of her mother, Belle. Helen G. Bonfils generously donated to hospitals, churches, and the theatre, building the Bonfils Theatre. This became the foundation for The Denver Center for the Performing Arts, one of the largest theatrical complexes in the United States.

MURIEL SIBELL WOLLE (1898-1977 New York, Colorado)

Muriel Sibell Wolle wrote six books for which she created thousands of sketches of Colorado's mining and ghost towns.

Daughter of an architect, Muriel grew up with an interest in buildings. As a tourist from New York in 1925, Muriel visited Central City, Colorado and vowed to return to sketch this mining city. One year later, she became assistant professor of Fine Arts at the University of Colorado, the department she headed from 1936 to 1947. Muriel returned to Central City often, sketching the entire city. She wanted to capture the sense of creaking boards and musty smells. Interested in the city's history, she interviewed residents, read old newspapers, and put the story and artwork into her first book, *Ghost Cities of Colorado*. Exploring and sketching Leadville resulted in her second book, *Cloud Cities*. While teaching and giving students a love of art, Muriel also designed the scenery and costumes for 90 plays of the university's Theatre Department. She married one of the founders of the theatre, English Professor Francis Wolle. For the next twenty years, they traveled by foot, horseback or jeep to about 240 mining communities of Colorado. Muriel sketched and researched mining/ghost towns, such as Breckenridge and Telluride. Her experiences and artwork became Professor Muriel Sibell Wolle's classic book, *Stampede to Timberline*, preserving through her creativity the ghost towns of Colorado.

ANTONIA BRICO (1902-1989 The Netherlands, California, New York, Colorado)

Dr. Antonia Brico was the first woman orchestra conductor in the United States and the conductor of the Brico Symphony in Denver for over thirty years.

With her foster parents, Antonia came to the United States in 1907. At age ten, she attended an outdoor band concert and was so inspired by the conductor of music that she decided this should be her life's career. Because no woman had ever been a conductor, all her teachers tried to discourage her. Antonia was focused on her goal. After six years of study, she graduated from the Master School of Conducting in Berlin, Germany. In 1930, Antonia Brico began her conducting career, leading the Berlin Philharmonic Orchestra. For the next seven years, Antonia was asked to conduct major orchestras throughout the United States. Gradually, the invitations stopped coming, perhaps because a woman orchestra conductor was no longer a novelty, or perhaps because of some people's prejudice against a woman in this role. In 1942, Antonia moved to Colorado and conducted the Denver Businessmen's Orchestra, which in 1969 was renamed the "Brico Symphony" in her honor. Because the orchestra played only five concerts a year, frustrated Antonia supported herself by teaching voice, piano, and conducting. One of her grateful students, folksinger Judy Collins, created an award-winning film about Antonia in 1974, reviving Antonia's career. Antonia Brico's talents as a conductor were once again shared with a world-wide audience.

MILDRED (BABE) DIDRIKSON ZAHARIAS (1911-1956 Texas, Colorado, Illinois, Florida)

"Babe" Didrikson Zaharias was one of the world's greatest women athletes. She set more records in a variety of sports than any other athlete, female or male, of the 20th century.

Known by her nickname, Babe was one of seven children to grow up in a loving family. Born with an ability to do well in sports, Babe's teenage goal was to become the greatest athlete that ever lived. At age eighteen, she became a one-person team in the 1932 national track and field championships. Entering eight events such as hurdles, high jump, broad jump, and javelin throwing, she won five events, placed in seven, and scored thirty points. The runner-up team, an entire club of women, scored only twenty-two points. In the 1932 Olympics, Babe won two gold medals for the 80-meter hurdles and javelin throw, setting new records. In 1935 she played her first golf game, driving the ball further than most long-time golfers: 240 yards. Babe loved golf and practiced daily, before and after work as well as at lunch time, on the office carpet. Even though her hands bled from so much practice, she continued. In one game, Babe realized she had been hitting a ball that was not hers. She disqualified herself knowing that good sportsmanship is as important as winning. She won most of the tournaments in which she played, including seventeen golf titles in a row. In 1947, she became the first American woman to win the British Women's Open. She and her Colorado born husband, George Zaharias, owned their first home in Denver. Babe Zaharias was inducted into the Colorado Women's Golf Hall of Fame.

RUTH MOSKO HANDLER (1916-   Colorado, California)

Ruth Handler, business genius and co-founder of Mattel Toy Company, created the world famous Barbie doll and Nearly Me products.

Ruth Mosko was the tenth and last child born to Polish parents who settled in Denver. Because of her mother's poor health, Ruth was lovingly raised from infancy to adulthood by her sister Sarah. Sarah provided a role model, which Ruth followed, of a woman working outside her home. Sarah at first disapproved of Ruth's love for Elliot Handler feeling that marriage to Elliot, an artist, would be a lifetime financial struggle. At age nineteen, Ruth moved to Los Angeles; Elliot followed and their extremely happy marriage has lasted nearly sixty years. Their business partnership began when Elliot created beautiful gift wear items which Ruth sold. Elliot began to design toys and they formed Mattel Toy Company in 1945. After watching daughter Barbara play with paper dolls, Ruth had the idea of creating an adult doll with many different outfits of clothing. She was told the doll would never sell, but Ruth Handler believed in her idea, was persistent and in 1959 the "Barbie" doll was born. Millions per year have been sold. The "Ken" doll, named for son Ken, arrived in 1961. Because of Ruth's talents in sales, marketing, and her good business sense, Mattel became the biggest toymaker in the world. After Ruth lost her breast to cancer, her new company, "Nearly Me," created artificial breasts, helping women who survived cancer.

DANA H. CRAWFORD (1931- Kansas, Colorado)

Dana H. Crawford is a a real estate developer who helped save Denver's past by preserving old buildings and giving them new life.

In 1858, General William E. Larimer, a founder of Denver, lived in one of the first cabins on Larimer Street. Other cabins and stores followed. One hundred years later, most of the late 1800's buildings were still standing, neglected and in a very run-down neighborhood. Dana Crawford, who loved history, had visited other cities which had restored their older buildings. In 1964, Dana had the idea of reviving Larimer Street, between 14th and 15th Streets. Almost every bank refused to loan her money. Dana persisted, and finally found financing. Dana, her husband, and an investor group purchased the old buildings on Larimer Street and hired people to repair them. Concrete pavement was replaced with brick and gas street lamps were installed. The newly renovated buildings were rented to restaurants, shops, and art galleries. Larimer Square was born and became one of Denver's most visited tourist spots. Dana encouraged people to live in lower downtown (LoDo) by renovating buildings for lofts and apartments, creating designer showrooms and bringing the Oxford Hotel back to its former beauty. In 1970, she helped found Historic Denver, Inc. to save the Molly Brown House. She also became active with The National Trust for Historic Preservation. Dana Crawford has shown that a good way to help cities is to combine preservation and business.

PATRICIA SCHROEDER (1940-   Oregon, Texas, Ohio, Iowa, Colorado, Washington, D.C.)

Patricia Schroeder, Denver's representative to the United States House of Representatives in Washington, D.C., had served longer in Congress than any other woman, twenty-four years. She has been a leader of children's and family issues throughout her career.

Because of her father's work, Pat had lived in six different cities by the time she graduated high school. A good student, Pat graduated from Harvard Law School, where she met fellow law student, Jim Schroeder, who became her husband. Jim, an encouraging husband, not only urged Pat to enter politics, but once she was elected, gave up his Denver law practice and became a Washington, D.C. lawyer. He was helpful in raising their children, then aged two and six. In 1973, the thirteen other women in Congress had no young children. Pat, a very organized person, managed being a wife, mother, and an active congressperson. As her children grew, they sometimes joined her on congressional travels and meetings. Pat Schroeder has great concern for the family and has helped pass laws which better protect children and strengthen the family, such as women's health research, violence against women, poor women's rights, and allowing parents to leave work for a short time to care for new babies or sick relatives. Pat was the first woman appointed to the Armed Services Committee and was inducted into The National Women's Hall of Fame. Pat was so well liked that she was re-elected to Congress every two years, a total of twelve times. She chose to retire in 1996 to continue her leadership in other directions.

JOYCE MESKIS (1942-   Illinois, Indiana, Colorado)

Joyce Meskis is the owner and developer of Tattered Cover Bookstore in Denver, one of the world's largest independent bookstores carrying half a million books.

Realizing that books were her passion, Joyce opened a small bookstore in Parker, Colorado. Because this community did not develop as planned, her bookstore failed. Joyce did not give up and purchased a small, three-year old bookstore in Denver, The Tattered Cover. Joyce's cozy store became so full of books and people that more space was needed. She made the daring decision to rent a four-story building a few blocks away. Her loyal customers carried books from the old to the new store. Customers feel trusted by Joyce's policy of accepting personal checks without a driver's license; they feel respected by the great efforts made to get a special order book. Joyce's employees are chosen because of their love and knowledge of books and authors. Joyce listens to her employees and acts on their good suggestions, making for a happy working environment. Joyce opened her first Tattered Cover with three employees; she now has 400 and two stores. Joyce Meskis encourages reading, knowing that ideas in books help people become more tolerant of different views. Some bookstores fear selling controversial books; Joyce Meskis believes in freedom of speech and courageously presents even unpopular books and authors, hoping for an open discussion and exchange of ideas.

JUDITH ALBINO (1943- Tennessee, New York, Colorado, California)

On June 1, 1991, Judith Albino became the first woman president of the University of Colorado, the largest university in the U.S. led by a woman.

When Judith was twelve years old, her father died. To support her family, Judith's mother went back to school, becoming a teacher. Judith learned from her mother that having an education helps one to become self-reliant. Judith was a professor and administrator at the State University of New York when she was asked to come to the University of Colorado as Vice President for Academic Affairs and Research. Judith accepted. One month later, the president of the university resigned. The Board of Regents rejected the search committee's choices for a new president and appointed Judith. After only eight months in Colorado, on June 1, 1991, Judith Albino became the first woman president in the 116-year history of the University of Colorado. Judith worked on university affairs until late every night, reserving Sundays to be with her husband Sal and two teen-age sons. She raised more money for the university than any previous president while increasing research and improving the quality of teaching for undergraduates. However, the elected Board of Regents and certain professors demanded Judith's resignation. Judith had the strength and determination to defy her critics, before resigning after four and a half years. Appreciated by others, she became president of a California school of higher education.

CLEO PARKER ROBINSON (1948 -   Colorado, Texas, Colorado)

Cleo Parker Robinson has achieved her vision of teaching dance to help young people discover their strengths. She is an inspirational master teacher, dancer, choreographer, and business person who created the world-class Cleo Parker Robinson Dance Ensemble. They have performed with theatre, operas, and symphonies in Colorado, throughout the United States and globally. Her international Colorado year-round school, three hundred seat theatre and at risk youth program are all housed in Denver's historic landmark, A.M.E. Shorter Church.

At age ten, Cleo almost died of heart failure and kidney disease. At first she was denied entrance into a Dallas, Texas hospital because of prejudice against African-Americans during the time of segregation in the U.S. Due to the life-threatening emergency, Cleo was admitted. Doctors told her she would be bed-ridden for life; Cleo was determined to actively use her body. As a high school student whose father was her first dance teacher, Cleo taught modern dance to university students. Finally she received formal dance training and was inspired by Arthur Mitchell who taught inner-city children in Harlem, New York. Cleo saw that students who often were abused or had drug and alcohol problems suddenly blossomed through dance. Cleo Parker decided her mission in life was to help people of all cultures, economic backgrounds and ages discover themselves through dance, music, and theatre. Returning to Denver, she became director of the Model Cities Cultural Center. In 1970, she married Tom Robinson and opened her first dance school, offering free lessons. No one came. Intent on her mission, Cleo visited schools trying to motivate future students to the magic of dance. Students who joined her experienced the joy of movement through dance. Today over ten thousand students have been taught by Cleo Parker Robinson, choreographer, dancer, and master teacher. Many have become great performers and successful in other professions; all have learned discipline, achieved self-esteem, and show compassion for others.

DOLORES S. ATENCIO (1955- Colorado)

In 1991, Dolores Atencio became the first Coloradan and second woman to be president of the Hispanic National Bar Association, an organization for Hispanic attorneys in the United States.

Dolores's mother worked long hours for low pay and experienced prejudice because of her dark skin. She encouraged Dolores to become an attorney to help fight injustice. Dolores achieved this goal by working hard for good grades and earning money for college and law school. Dolores became so interested in Colorado's first Hispanic radio station, KUVO, which her friend Florence Hernandez-Rámos was forming, that she left her job with the attorney general to work there full time. When KUVO began in 1985, Dolores handled its legal work, fund raising and public relations. When her daughter was born, she did part-time legal work at home. She later worked for the Colorado Bar Association, where she helped organize the first Colorado minority women lawyers conference in 1989. Believing that women need to be leaders, she ran for president of the Hispanic National Bar Association (HNBA) and won the election. Dolores Atencio became the second woman and first Coloradan to hold this office. Under Dolores' leadership, the lack of Hispanic federal judges was noticed. She worked hard to see that Hispanic judges were recognized and appointed to the federal courts. Some of them were women. In 1997, Dolores Atencio's strengths as an attorney and leader resulted in her becoming the first Hispanic woman administrative law judge for the state of Colorado.

LINDA ALVARADO   (1951-   New Mexico, California, Colorado)

Linda Alvarado is president of Alvarado Construction, Inc., one of the largest construction companies in the United States owned by a woman. She is also the first Hispanic to be a part owner of a major league baseball team, The Colorado Rockies.

Linda was the only girl in a family of six children. Her parents encouraged her in school and athletics. She did well in both, gaining much self-confidence. After college in California, Linda and her husband Robert Alvarado moved to Colorado. Linda had worked in construction management and wanted to start her own general contracting business. Her parents so strongly believed in Linda, that they borrowed money to help Linda with her goal. Under Linda's management, the company started pouring concrete foundation walls and floors for buildings. Eventually, as a large general contractor, Alvarado Construction, Inc., built the Colorado Convention Center, a nine-story building for U.S. West Communications in Inverness Park, the Naval Marine Reserve, the Burnsley Hotel, and Concourse B at Stapleton International Airport. With another company, Alvarado Construction, Inc. is building the aquarium, Colorado's Ocean Journey. Linda is committed to quality, safety, and completing a job on schedule. She also finds time for civic and charitable organizations. In 1996, Linda Alvarado became chairperson of the board of directors of the Denver Hispanic Chamber of Commerce. She was a founder of the Committee of 200, a national group of business women, and was president of the Women's Forum of Colorado. *Hispanic Business Magazine* named her one of the "100 Most Influential Hispanics in America."

AMY VAN DYKEN   (1973-   Colorado)

Amy Van Dyken became the first American woman to win four gold medals in a single Olympics, Atlanta, 1996.

At eighteen months old, Amy was diagnosed with asthma, a lung disease which makes breathing very difficult. Asthma attacks can be caused by too much exercise, infections, or allergies. All three affected Amy and still do to this day. Because of her asthma, Amy could not play active childhood games. She could not visit the zoo because an asthma attack could occur. Amy's doctors suggested she try swimming to develop her lungs. At first, she hardly had the lung power to cross the pool. By age twelve, this goal was reached, although she was always the last out of the pool in any race. She was so slow, her high-school teammates refused to swim a relay race if Amy Van Dyken was on the team. This, as well as the teasing she received for being six feet tall, hurt Amy. Amy's parents and friends encouraged her; others did not. Amy did not listen to the people who said she was not an athlete; she just tried harder. Amy's years of practice and great determination amazingly resulted in her winning state championships, setting Colorado state records and qualifying for the 1996 Olympics. With medicine for her asthma, she could breathe with 65% of her lung power. Amy Van Dyken, using all her physical and mental strength, won the top prize in four separate swim events.....four gold medals!

LISTS OF ACHIEVEMENTS

The next pages list the names and accomplishments made by women who either were born in Colorado, lived in Colorado, worked in Colorado, or helped the people of Colorado. The women were selected based on their names appearing in many sources. Some of the women were not fully appreciated in their day; others received numerous awards and honors, most not listed here. The work of some women overlaps into different career categories. The states listed after the years of birth and death of each woman represent the place of birth and other states in which each woman has lived. All careers and "firsts" for women were not possible for the scope of this book; only a broad overview was intended. The author of this book knows there are many omissions due to space limitations; however, readers are encouraged to submit names and missing information which will be considered for future printings.

THE ARTS
ACTOR, TELEVISION PERSONALITY, PERFORMING ARTS, THEATRE DIRECTOR/PRODUCER

Maude Fealy   (1881-1971 Tennessee, Colorado, California)
Maude Fealy acted in theatre from Elitch's to London.

Antoinette Perry   (1888-1946 Colorado, New York)
Theatre's Tony Award is given for the best plays, actors, writers, directors. The award was named for Antoinette Perry, theatre actor, director, president of Experimental Theatre, Inc. and chair of the American Theatre Wing.

Spring Byington   (1893-1971 Colorado, New York)
Spring Byington was a television actor and appeared in over ninety films.

Hanya Holm   (c.1898-1992 Germany, Colorado, New York)
Modern dance teacher and choreographer Hanya Holm choreographed Broadway theatrical shows such as *My Fair Lady*, *Camelot* and *Kiss Me Kate*. She taught a summer dance workshop at Colorado College in Colorado Springs for more than forty years, 1941-1983.

Hattie McDaniel   (1895-1952 Kansas, Colorado)
Hattie McDaniel was the first African-American to win an Academy Award. She won it for her role as "Mammy" in *Gone With The Wind*.

Lucy M. Walker   (1927- Tennessee, Colorado)
Lucy M. Walker founded the multi-cultural Eden Theatrical Workshop in 1963. This is the longest continuously running arts organization started by an African-American woman.

Reynelda Muse   (1946- Ohio, Colorado)
African-American, Reynelda Muse, was the first woman to anchor television news in Colorado, beginning in 1968. For over four years she was one of the original anchors for the Cable News Network (CNN) and then returned to Denver's KCNC, Channel 4 television. Reynelda Muse was the first woman selected *Broadcaster of the Year* by the Colorado Broadcasters Association.

Bertha Lynn   (Germany, Washington, Colorado)
Since 1976, Bertha Lynn has reported Colorado news as a reporter and anchor with 7 News, KMGH-TV. Prior to that, she was at Channel 9, KUSA. She also hosted a community affairs program for KRMA, public television. Active in many Denver organizations, Bertha Lynn has received numerous awards: *Best On-Air Personality* by the National Academy of Television Arts & Sciences, Colorado Chapter, and as an African-American, *Journalist of the Year* in Broadcasting from the Colorado Association of Black Journalists.

Beverly Martinez   (1946- Colorado, New Jersey, Colorado)
In 1973, Beverly Martinez was hired by Channel 2 to host a local talk show, *Denver Now*. She became the first Hispanic woman to host her own talk show nationally. Today she is KWGN's Community Relations Manager.

Roseanne   (1952- Utah, Colorado, California)
Comedian Roseanne performed her first professional comedy routines in Denver nightclubs, where in 1983 she was known as the "Queen of Denver Comedy." Three years after her move to Los Angeles, her television show, *Roseanne*, debuted in October, 1988. It became the number one rated television show by October 1989. She has won Emmy, Golden Globe and People's Choice awards and continues to entertain the public in both series and television specials. Roseanne has shared her life in two autobiographies.

ANTHROPOLOGISTS

Hannah Marie Wormington   (1914-1994 Colorado, Arizona, Colorado, Minnesota, Wyoming, Colorado)
    Hannah Marie Wormington was the first curator of archeology at the Denver Museum of Natural History, a position she held for thirty-two years until 1968. She taught in several universities and wrote many books and articles about ancient people of Central and South America. Hannah Marie Wormington was the first woman to receive a doctoral degree in anthropology from Harvard University and first woman to become president of the Society for American Archeology.

ARCHITECTS

Elizabeth Wright Ingraham   (1922- Indiana, Colorado)
    At the age of thirteen, Elizabeth knew she wanted to become an architect while visiting the studio of her grandfather, the great architect, Frank Lloyd Wright. She entered a field in which there were very few women. She designed buildings, founded a school, guided young architects, and answered many questions about her grandfather. Elizabeth Wright Ingraham was the first Colorado woman to be admitted as a Fellow to the American Institute of Architects.

Patricia O'Leary   (Illinois, Arkansas, Colorado)
    In 1996, Professor Patricia O'Leary was the first woman appointed Dean of the College of Architecture and Planning at the University of Colorado, Denver, in charge of both the Denver and Boulder campuses.

Jane Silverstein Ries   (1909- Colorado)
    Denver's first woman landscape architect was Jane Silverstein Ries. For over sixty years, she has designed landscapes for private homes and public places such as the Governor's Mansion, Denver's Botanic Gardens, schools, banks and hospitals.

ARTISTS
Creating Paintings, Water Colors, Sculptures, Photographs, Murals, Ceramics, Needlework

Eliza Greatorex   (1819-1897 Ireland, New York, Colorado, France)
    In 1873, a book publishing company sent Eliza Greatorex to Colorado Springs to create sketches for the book *Summer Etchings in Colorado*. She became the first professional woman artist in Colorado Springs.

Mary Elizabeth Achey   (1832-1886 Scotland or Germany, Colorado, California, Washington)
    Mary Elizabeth Achey was Colorado's first professional woman artist, working in Central City, Colorado from 1860-1869. She created over 500 paintings, drawings, needleworks, and wood engravings, while being the sole support of her two sons.

Harriet Hayden   (1840-1906 Massachusetts, Illinois, Colorado)
    In 1890, The Le Brun Art Club, named for the French portrait painter Elisabeth Vigee Le Brun, was begun by Harriet Hayden in her studio. The Club became The Artists Club of Denver and eventually became The Denver Art Museum.

Helen Lynch Dill   (1848-1928   Vermont, New York, Colorado)
    On a school teacher's salary, Helen Dill made such good real estate investments, that she became very wealthy. The money she donated in her will to the Denver Art Museum was used to purchase over thirty-seven works of art which are considered to be among the most valued of the museum. The museum's Helen Dill Society encourages the generosity of other donors.

Helen Chain   (1848-1892   Indiana, Colorado)
    Helen Chain painted landscapes in oil and watercolor. The modern art gallery she and her husband owned was one of the few places where Denver artists could exhibit.

Anne Lodge Parrish   (c. 1850-?   ?, Pennsylvania, Colorado, ?)
    From 1880 to 1900/1903, portrait painter Ann Lodge Parrish and her husband Thomas Parrish began the first art school in Colorado Springs.

Alice Stewart Hill   (1850-c.1921 Wisconsin, Colorado)
    Alice Stewart Hill painted Colorado flowers and still lifes and illustrated Helen Hunt Jackson's book, *Procession of the Flowers of Colorado*.

Emma Richardson Cherry   (1859-1954 Illinois, Colorado, Texas)
    In 1893, the first meeting of the Artists' Club of Denver was held in Emma Richardson Cherry's studio. The Artists' Club of Denver became the Denver Art Association and then became The Denver Art Museum. Emma Richardson Cherry was the first art teacher at the University of Denver.

Elizabeth Henrietta Bromwell   (1859-1946 Illinois, Colorado)
    Landscape painter, Elizabeth Henrietta Bromwell, was a founding member of The Artists' Club of Denver in 1893. It later became The Denver Art Museum.

Charlotte Jane Whitehead   (1866-1964 Kansas, Colorado)
    Beginning at age sixty-three, Charlotte Jane Whitehead produced over thirty-five museum quality quilts, many now owned by The Denver Art Museum.

Elisabeth Spalding   (1868-1954 Pennsylvania, Colorado)
    A landscape and flower painter in oil, watercolor and pastel, Denver artist Elisabeth Spalding was also a strong supporter of the newly formed Denver Art Museum.

Nellie Walker   (1874-1973 Iowa, Illinois, Colorado)
    Colorado Springs sculptor, Nellie Walker, created bronze statues and memorials, such as that of charitable Winfield Scott Stratton of Colorado Springs. She was four feet ten inches tall and stood on ladders to create her larger than life-size sculptures.

Mabel Landrum Torrey (1886-1974 Colorado, Illinois, Iowa)
   Mabel Landrum Torrey created the nineteen ton marble sculpture of *Wynken, Blynken, and Nod* located in Denver's Washington Park. It is based on Eugene Field's poem.

Laura Gilpin (1891-1979 Colorado, New Mexico)
   Photographer Laura Gilpin's black and white images are found in U.S. museum collections. Her books about the South West, accompanied by her photos, won many awards.

Irene Stein (1894- Colorado)
   At age 84, Irene Stein wore goggles, a hard hat, and used a torch to create her metal sculptures. She has worked in many mediums: plastic, metal, printmaking.

Eve Drewelowe (1899-1988 Iowa, Colorado)
   Eve Drewelowe was the first person to receive a master of fine arts degree from the University of Iowa and the first woman to have a solo exhibiton of her work in Boulder, Colorado. She was one of the founders of the Boulder Artists Guild. Many of her 1000 paintings, drawings and sculptures represent her love of the Rocky Mountains and concern for damage to the environment.

Louise Ronnebeck (1901-1980 Pennsylvania, New York, Colorado, Bermuda)
   Louise Ronnebeck came to Denver in 1926 when her husband Arnold Ronnebeck, a sculptor, was appointed director of the Denver Art Museum. She created murals and frescos (paint on plaster) for post offices and other public places in Colorado and Wyoming. She taught drawing and painting at the University of Denver, 1945-1950.

Gladys Caldwell Fisher (1907-1952 Colorado)
   Gladys Caldwell Fisher was a sculptor in stone and wood, specializing in animals. She created two mountain sheep for the entrance of Denver's former Main Post Office on 18th Street between Champa and Stout streets, which today is the Byron White United States Courthouse. She often sketched wild animals, locked with them in their cages, but was never injured by an animal.

Nadine Drummond (1912-1966 Colorado)
   Colorado Springs Fine Arts Center teacher, Nadine Drummond expressed what she loved in her paintings: Southern Colorado, skiing, hiking, outdoor life. Some of her paintings depict the great problems of Colorado farmers in the 1930s: dust storms, drought, fields ruined by grasshoppers.

Nan Bangs McKinnell (1913-   Nebraska, Washington, Maryland, Colorado, Washington, Montana, Massachusetts,
New Hampshire, Iowa, New York, Iowa, Japan, Scotland, Colorado)
   From 1954 to 1955, Nan Bangs McKinnell and husband Jim McKinnell made major improvements to the kiln, the oven used to bake their ceramic creations. Nan Bangs McKinnell taught at many universities in the U.S., Japan, and Scotland, as well as Loretto Heights College.

Ethel Magafan (1916-1933 Illinois, Colorado, New York)
   New York's Metropolitan Museum of Art and The Denver Art Museum are among the many places which own paintings by Ethel Magafan. She and her twin sister Jenne Magafan (1916-1952), with government support, created large murals for post offices in Colorado, Nebraska, Araknsas, and Oklahoma.

Mary Chenoweth (1918-   New York, Illinois, Colorado, Nebraska)
   Art professor Mary Chenoweth is a painter and print-maker. For thirty years from 1953 to 1983, she taught these art forms, influencing students at Colorado College, in Colorado Springs.

Eppie Archuletta (1922- New Mexico, Colorado)
   Learning the art of blanket weaving from her Native American grandfather, Eppie Archuletta wove rugs and blankets. Through Adams State College in Alamosa, Colorado, Eppie Archuletta taught weaving to other adults. Her work can be seen at The Smithsonian Institute in Washington, D.C. The National Endowment for the Arts called her a "national treasure."

Glenna Goodacre (1939- Texas, Colorado, New Mexico)
   1994 was the dedication of the Vietnam Women's Memorial designed by Glenna Goodacre. It is located on the Mall in Washington, D.C. Learning about the competition for this memorial only ten days before the deadline, she quickly entered drawings and a small clay model. She won the competition.   Years before, her college sculpture teacher gave her the grade of D. Glenna Goodacre never sculpted and only created paintings with oils, pastels and water colors. Fifteen years later, an encouraging gallery owner gave her wax to create a sculpture, and turned it into bronze. This changed Glenna Goodacre's life. She has since created many larger-than-life sculptures.

Ruth Thorne-Thomsen (1943- New York, California, Illinois, Colorado, Pennsylvania)
   Ruth Thorne-Thomsen's black and white photographs can be found in collections all over the world.

Carlota D. Espinoza (1943- Colorado)
   Eleventh generation Coloradan, Carlotta Espinoza, is part Spanish, Ute Indian, Aztec, and Italian. Carlota D. Espinoza is often thought to be the finest mural painter and diorama creator in the western U.S. One of her dioramas (painted background scenes) is the Cheyenne Native American group at the Denver Museum of Natural History, where she worked for nine years. Other murals may be seen at the state Historical Museum, churches, schools, libraries in Colorado, Arizona, and California.

Kay Miller (1946- Texas, Ohio, Nebraska, Iowa, Colorado)
   Professor of Fine Arts at the University of Colorado, Kay Miller's works are spriritual using symbols.

Veryl Goodnight (1947-   Colorado, New Mexico)
   Veryl Goodnight's sculptures of western women and animals are located in world-wide collections and in the Denver Zoo, the Pro-Rodeo Hall of Fame, Colorado Springs, the National Cowboy Hall of Fame, Oklahoma, and in the Bush Presidential Library, Texas.

BANKING/FINANCE

LaRae Orullian (1933- Utah, Colorado)
LaRae Orullian was a founder, the first president, and CEO of The Women's Bank, Denver, Colorado. From 1990-1996, she served as president of the Girl Scouts of the USA. LaRae Orullian is chair of The Women's Bank and the first woman chair of Frontier Airlines.

Barbara Grogan (1947- Missouri, Colorado)
Barbara Grogan was the first woman chair of the Federal Reserve Bank, Denver branch, 1988, first woman president of the Denver Metropolitan Chamber of Commerce, 1992-1993, and is president of Western Industrial Contractors.

Nancy McCallin (Colorado)
Since 1989, the first chief economist of the Colorado Legislative Council has been economist, Nancy McCallin, Ph.D. The Council gives research information to the legislators so they can make good decisions about Colorado's budget.

Linda Petty (1950- Iowa, Florida, Iowa, Colorado)
Linda Petty became the first woman chair of the Colorado Bankers Association, 1997.

Barbara Walker (1953- Colorado)
Barbara Walker became Colorado's first woman State Banking Commissioner in 1991, and the first woman executive director of the Independent Banks of Colorado, 1997.

Jo Marie Dancik (1956- Japan, Ohio, Virginia, Ohio, Colorado)
Jo Marie Dancik is the deputy chair of the Kansas City Federal Reserve Bank Board. She is the first woman to be a managing partner in any office and first woman manager of the Denver office of Ernst and Young, the world's second largest accounting and tax firm. In 1995, Jo Marie Dancik became the first woman, since the founding of Mile High United Way in 1887 by Florence Wisebart Jacobs, to chair the Metro Denver campaign.

BUSINESS OWNERS/BUSINESS PROMOTERS

Millie Booth (1837-1926 Pennsylvania, Wisconsin, New Mexico, Colorado)
Gold mining brought Millie Booth and her husband to Colorado in 1860. In 1864, they bought the Four Mile Stage Stop. As trains replaced stage coaches, they purchased up to 600 acres of land. Mille Booth and her family became dairy farmers and bee keepers for almost 60 years. Four Mile Historic Park at 715 So. Forest, Denver, is a museum of the Booth home, farm, and stage coach.

Ellen E. Jack (Captain Jack) (1842- England, Colorado)
Ellen Jack, known as Captain Jack, was a mine owner and pioneer prospector in Gunnison, Crested Butte, and Aspen.

Elizabeth Fuller Iliff Warren (1845-1920 Illinois, Colorado)
At age 24, Elizabeth came to Colorado by stagecoach to sell sewing machines. She married John Wesley Iliff, and after his death, managed their huge cattle business. She generously donated money to the University of Denver to begin the Iliff School of Theology.

Nora Gaines (c.1863-c.1933 Michigan, Colorado)
Nora competed in a man's profession, driving a team of horses as a Colorado tourist guide in Colorado Springs.

Madame C.J. Walker (1867-1919 Louisiana, Mississippi, Missouri, New York, Colorado)
Aftrican-American Madame C.J. Walker became the first self-made woman millionaire in the U.S. through her business of creating beauty products for African-Americans. She employed 2000 women to sell her products door to door.

Olga Little (1883-1970 Germany, Colorado)
From 1901 to 1947, Olga Little ran the only burro pack train in the United States. Her burros came down the mountain loaded with ore from the mines and returned up the mountain with mining supplies.

Kathryn Hach-Darrow (1922- Missouri, Iowa, Colorado)
Kathryn Hach-Darrow is the only woman to head one of the largest companies in Colorado. She is the CEO and majority stock holder in the publicly held Hach Company, which she and her husband Cliff Hach founded in 1948 in Ames, Iowa. Their company moved to Loveland, Colorado in 1978. The company applies analytical chemistry to test drinking water, waste water, and industrial waters as well as performing soil and agricultural analyses.

Clara Villarosa (1930- Illinois, Colorado)
In Denver in 1984, Clara Villarosa opened the largest African-American bookstore in the U.S, the Hue-Man Experience Bookstore. She volunteers her time to encourage reading in schools and prisons, and holds small-business seminars for the African-American community. In 1994, Clara Villarosa was named Minority Entrepreneur of the Year by the U.S. Commerce Department.

Jo Farrell (1932- Michigan, Wyoming, Colorado, California, Colorado)
Jo Farrell founded JF Talent, a business which helped discover new actors and models. Jo Farrell teaches students to face and overcome their fears and to focus on their positive talents.

Gwendolyn Mayo 1932- Minnesota, Colorado)
Gwendolyn Mayo is chairperson, owner and founder of Mayo Aviation, Inc., an aircraft charter company based at Centennial Airport in Colorado. Seventeen aircraft, including six jets, form this largest airplane charter company between Chicago and Los Angeles. Gwendolyn Mayo, Ph.D. in organic research chemistry, was also the first woman chairperson of the National Air Transportation Association.

Yrma Rico (1940's- Texas, California, Rhode Island, Texas, Colorado)
Yrma Rico is the first Hispanic woman in Colorado to be general manager of a television station. She has been in this industry for twenty years. KCEC Channel 50 is an all Spanish language station, airing in Denver, Colorado Springs, and Pueblo.

Patricia Barella Rivera (1947- New Mexico, Colorado)
Patricia Barella Rivera is Colorado's first woman and first U.S. Latina to be appointed District Director for the State of Colorado's Small Business Administration.

Florence Hernandez-Rámos (1950- Colorado)
Florence Hernandez-Rámos is the first Hispanic female president and general manager of a public radio station in Denver. KUVO, 89.3 FM, began in 1985 as Denver's first bilingual radio station. Florence Hernandez-Rámos organized, raised funds, gathered a board of directors, installed broadcasting equipment and created an award winning Hispanic station.

Jane Withers (1952- Pennsylvania, Florida, The Netherlands, Georgia, Louisiana, Arkansas, Colorado)
Jane Withers, a former registered nurse, overcame an addiction to drugs and alcohol. She had been arrested many times by the police. Today she owns and runs the largest used hub cap business in the U.S., Hub Cap Annie. Jane Withers gives many inspirational public talks on drug rehabilitation, achievement, and her unique business. In 1988, she became the first president of the Colorado Women's Chamber of Commerce, which she and nine other Denver area businesswomen founded.

Anna Garcia (1953- Colorado, California, Ohio, Colorado)
In 1981, Anna Garcia began her steel company, Anko Metals. She is the first and only woman CEO in the steel industry in Colorado.

Sharon Vigil (1954- Colorado)
In 1996, Sharon Vigil became the first woman president of the Hispanic Chamber of Commerce in Denver which was founded in 1978.

Saba Jalil (1965- Pakistan, England, New York, Colorado)
Saba Jalil is the first woman president and board chair of the Asian Chamber of Commerce. She is president and one of the founders of Colorado 8(a), a federal program helping minority businesses become certified.

DIRECTORS/MANAGERS

Helen Black (1896-1988 Washington, D.C., Colorado)
Helen Black was the first woman to become manager of a U.S. symphony, The Denver Symphony, from 1945 to 1964. She was one of three founders of The Denver Symphony, working as an unpaid volunteer from 1933 to 1945. She booked the auditorium, handled ticket sales, dealt with guest artists, and had a full-time advertising job for a department store. In the 1930s, Helen Black helped revive the Central City Opera and volunteered as publicity manager until 1947.

Joyce Davies (1926- Rhode Island, Maine, Colorado)
Joyce Davies was one of the founders of Historic Boulder and its first president in 1972. Historic Boulder helps to preserve the past in Boulder, often saving buildings from being torn down.

Toni Dewey (1928- Illinois, Colorado)
In 1991, Toni Dewey, a retired corporate vice president of Motorola, Inc., founded the Women of the West Museum, known as WOW. The museum, to be located in Boulder, Colorado, will trace and interpret the history of women of all cultures in the American West, from earliest times to the present.

Maggie Divelbiss (1930's- New York, Colorado)
Maggie Divelbiss is the first woman director of Pueblo, Colorado's Sangre de Cristo Arts and Conference Center, the largest arts facility in southeast Colorado.

Barbara Sutteer (1940- Utah, Arizona, New Mexico, Alaska, Montana, Colorado)
Northern Ute and Cherokee American Indian, Barbara Sutteer was the first American Indian and first woman superintendent of the Little Big Horn Battle Field National Monument in Montana, 1989-1993. She now is the American Indian liason for the National Parks and American Indian Tribes for the states of Montana, Wyoming, Colorado and Utah. This includes such parks as Yellowstone, Glacier, and the Grand Tetons.

Polly Baca (1941- Colorado, Washington D.C., Arizona, Washington, D.C., Colorado)
Polly Baca is the first woman regional administrator for the General Services Administration. She is in charge of U.S. government buildings and work environment for a six-state area. From 1989 to 1993, she was the executive director of the Colorado Institute for Hispanic Education and Economic Development. (please see more under political)

Jean Trombley (1945- Iowa, Nebraska, Colorado)
Jean Trombley is the first director of the Denver Victims Service Center which was founded in 1987. Free support, crisis intervention, and counseling are given to victims of crime, most of whom are women. The excellent programs created in Denver have been chosen by the federal government to be a national model.

Kathyrn (Kate) Paul (1946- Pennsyslvania, New York, California, Colorado, Connecticut, Ohio, Colorado)
The Kaiser Foundation Health Plan of Colorado is an organization which provides health care insurance for people. Kaiser Foundation has six U.S. divisions. Since 1994 Kathryn Paul has been its first and only woman division president, in charge of the Rocky Mountain region.

Kerry Kramer (1947- Kansas, North Carolina, Illinois, Colorado)
From 1981 to 1987, Kerry Kramer was the first woman director of the El Pueblo Museum in Pueblo, Colorado. This is a regional museum of the Colorado Historical Society, founded in 1953.

Susan Engfer (Minnesota, Michigan, Wyoming, California, Colorado)
There are very few women in the U.S. who are directors of zoos. Since 1988, Susan Engfer has been the first woman director of the The Cheyenne Mountain Zoo in Colorado Springs, created by Spencer Penrose in 1926.

Lark Birdsong (1951- Kansas, Oklahoma, North Carolina, Iowa, Colorado)
Lark Birdsong is the first woman general manager of the Colorado Xplosion, a woman's professional basketball team.

Lisa Harjo (1952- Oklahoma, Colorado, Wyoming, Utah, California, Colorado)
Since 1983, Choctaw Native American, Lisa Harjo, has been the executive director of Denver Indian Center, Inc.

Deborah Jordy (1953- Colorado, California, England, France, Colorado)
Deborah Jordy is the first woman executive director of the Arvada Center for the Arts and Humanities.

Corinne C. Nystrom (1954- Colorado)
Corinne C. Nystrom is the first woman to manage Grand Junction's airport.

Raylene Decatur (1956- Virginia, Washington, D.C., Pennsylvania, Maryland, Colorado)
Raylene Decatur is the first woman president and CEO of the Denver Museum of Natural History.

Carol Jean Brafford (1959- South Dakota, North Dakota, Arizona, California, New Mexico, Montana, Arizona, Wyoming, Colorado)
Oglala Sioux Native American and anthropologist, "C.J." Brafford, in 1996 was the first American Indian to be appointed director of the Ute Indian Museum in Montrose, Colorado. From 1988 to 1995, she was the first American Indian to be curator of Wyoming's Grand Teton National Park.

Jessie Roberson (1958- Alabama, Tennessee, Georgia, South Carolina, Colorado)
Jessie Roberson, a nuclear engineer, is the only woman to head the 5,000 employee Rocky Flats federal facility, where nuclear warheads were made until 1989. A college professor told Jessie that she did not deserve to be in engineering. That remark made African-American Jessie Roberson determined to succeed as an engineer.

Ellen Robinson (1962- Massachusetts, Pennsylvania, Texas, Colorado)
Ellen Robinson is president of Ascent Sports, Inc., which manages both the Colorado Avalanche and the Denver Nuggets. She is one of only two women in the U.S. in this leadership position. Before this, Ellen Robinson was the general manager of Denver's Pepsi Cola Bottling Company.

EDUCATION
Many people thought girls and women did not need a formal education, as their roles were to be homemakers. The law makers of Colorado did not agree. The 1881 Colorado Constitution stated that "every child from ages six to eighteen years old shall attend school."

Ione Hanna (1837-1924 ? Colorado)
Ione Hanna was the first Colorado woman elected to a public office, serving on the Denver school board, 1893. (please see political)

Grace Espy Patton (1866- Pennsylvania, Colorado)
Three years after Ione Hanna was elected, Grace Espy Patton, professor at Colorado State University, Ft. Collins, was elected state superintendent of public instruction. She was co-editor of *The Colorado Woman*, a journal on women's rights which helped women become educated voters.

Anna Wolcott Vaile (1858-1928 Rhode Island, Colorado)
Anna Wolcott Vaile was the principal of the Denver private school, Wolfe Hall from 1892 to 1898. She then founded and became principal of Wolcott School for Girls in Denver. In 1910, she became the first woman to be elected regent of the University of Colorado. Anna Wolcott Vaile was director of the School of American Archaeology and vice-president of the Colorado Society of the American Institute of Archaeology.

Mary Ripon (1850-1935 Illinois, Germany, France, Switzerland, Michigan, Colorado)
Mary Ripon became one of the first women in the U.S. to teach in a state university when hired as a professor for the University of Colorado's beginning year, 1878. She was head of the department of Germanic languages and literature until her retirement in 1909. In gratitude, the university named their outdoor theatre for her.

Lois Jones Shepard (c.1852-1918 Kentucky, Missouri, Colorado, Illinois)
Lois Jones Shepard was the first woman elected superintendent of schools for Pueblo, Colorado, 1898.

Nettie Shwer Freed (c.1881-1979 Ohio, Colorado, Utah, Colorado)
In 1946, Nettie Schwer Freed of Pueblo, Colorado, became the first Colorado commissioner of education. Until 1948, this position was called state superintendent of public school education. (please see political)

Pauline Robinson (1915-1997 Oklahoma, Colorado)
Pauline Robinson had several firsts as an African-American woman in the Denver Public Library system: first librarian hired, 1943; first to become a supervisor, in her case head of Childrens' Services; first branch manager; and first childrens' services coordinator, in charge of the childrens' services for all twenty-one branches and the main Denver Public Library. The Robinson Library at 5575 East 33rd Avenue, Denver, was named in appreciation of her.

Rachel Bassette Noel (1918- Virginia, Tennessee, Washington, D.C., Virginia, Arizona, California, Missouri, Colorado)
In 1965, Rachel Noel was the first black woman elected to the Denver School Board. She worked hard and long in support of equal education for all children, resulting in the desegregation of the Denver Public Schools. She was appointed to the board and then elected president of the University of Colorado Board of Regents. Rachel Bassette Noel is the retired chair of African-American studies at Metropolitan State College.

Evie Dennis (1924- Mississippi, Missouri, Colorado)
Dr. Evie Dennis, whose doctorate is in education, was the first woman and the first black American to become superintendent of the Denver Public Schools, 1990-1994. She was vice president of the U.S. Olympic Committee, 1980-1988, and is now special assistant to the president of the U.S. Olympic Committee.

Bea Romer (1929- Wyoming, Colorado)
Bea Romer, wife of Colorado Governor Roy Romer, has a masters degree in educational psychology. She is a leader in the field of family and children's health issues. She is chairperson of the Colorado Initiative for Family Learning, is involved in Bright Beginnings, a Colorado project which helps communities organize support for new families, and serves on national boards protecting children.

Elnora M. Gilfoyle (1934- Iowa, Colorado)
Dr. Elnora Gilfoyle was an occupational therapy professor, the dean, first woman provost, and academic vice president of Colorado State University. Because of the programs she developed, CSU has become one of the top schools in the nation in occupational therapy.

Jessica Marie Luna (1936-1982 Colorado)
Active community volunteer in Pueblo, Colorado, Jessica Marie Luna was a co-founder of the Denver Children's Museum.

Kaye Howe (1938- Pennsylvania, Illinois, Ohio, West Virginia, Florida, Georgia, Texas, Missouri, Wyoming, Colorado)
Kaye Howe was the first woman president of Western State College in Gunnison, Colorado, serving from 1991 to 1996. She now is the first woman president of the International University, an internet/web university where all classes are taught on the web.

Mary Frances Berry (1939- Maryland, Colorado, Washington, D.C., ?)
Mary Frances Berry, Ph.D., attorney and author, became the first woman and first African-American chancellor of the University of Colorado, 1976 to 1977. In 1977 she became assistant secretary for education in the Department of Health, Education, and Welfare.

Georgia E. Lesh-Laurie (1938- Ohio, Wisconsin, Ohio, New York, Ohio, Colorado)
Georgia E. Lesh-Laurie, Ph.D., is the first woman to head the University of Colorado at Denver (UCD) as chancellor. She is a developmental biologist and has been vice chancellor of academic and student affairs at UCD and an interim vice president at Cleveland State University.

Irene I. Blea (1946- New Mexico, Colorado, New Mexico, California)
Ph.D., Irene I. Blea, was the first woman chair of any Chicano studies department in the nation, at Denver's Metropolitan State College. In the early 1970's, she was part of a committee which designed a Chicano studies program for the state of Colorado. From this group developed the National Association of Chicano Studies with Dr. Irene I. Blea its first woman national chair in 1978.

Mary Grace Jarvis (1948- Missouri, Colorado)
Mary Grace Jarvis is the first Coloradan to be selected National 1996 Principal of the Year by the National Association of Secondary School Principals and Met Life Insurance Co. She is the principal of Smoky Hill High School in the Cherry Creek School District, Aurora, Colorado.

Jane Hammond (1948- Maryland, Texas, North Carolina, Washington, Colorado)
In 1997, Jane Hammond became the first woman superintendent of schools for Colorado's largest school district, Jefferson County, after its re-organization in the 1950's.

FIREFIGHTERS
Heather Larson (1951- Illinois, Colorado)
Linda Smith Mangels (1956- Colorado)
Heather Larson and Linda Smith Mangels became Denver's first women firefighters in 1985. They filed a sex discrimination complaint after they were turned down for firefighter jobs because they failed a physical fitness test. There was a settlement and both Lieutenant Larson and Firefighter Mangels are now active and effective firefighters.

JUDICIAL and LEGAL CAREERS

When the Honorable Zita L. Weinshienk (see below) finished Harvard Law School, her class of 489 students had only six women graduates. In the 1990s, 40% to 50% of the law school students are women. In 1958, Judge Weinshienk's law school dean told the women students that he thought they might all get married, have children, and not use their Harvard education. Years later, the dean told Judge Weinshienk that he had been wrong. Women graduates throughout the United States had written to him of their successful careers in law, and they were usually also wives and mothers.

JUDGES

Irena S. Ingham (1900- ? Colorado, ?)
Irena Ingham of Cripple Creek, Colorado, was the first woman district court judge in Colorado, appointed to the fourth judicial district, 1938.

Aurel M. Kelly (1923- Ohio, Washington, Colorado)
In 1974, Aurel M. Kelly became the first woman to serve on the Colorado Court of Appeals. She became its first woman chief judge in 1988.

Patti F. O'Rourke (1923- New York, Colorado)
Patti F. O'Rourke became Pueblo, Colorado's first woman district court judge in 1981. She now serves as a senior district judge.

Zita L. Weinshienk (1933- Minnesota, Arizona, Colorado)
Zita L. Weinshienk became the first woman United States district court judge for the District of Colorado, beginning in 1979. She was the first woman district judge appointed in the Tenth Circuit, which includes six states: Colorado, Utah, New Mexico, Kansas, Oklahoma, and Wyoming. Before that she was the first Denver woman to be a judge in various courts: state district court judge, 1972-1979; county court judge, 1965-1971; municipal court judge, 1964-1965. She was a referee in Juvenile Court, 1959-1964.

Jean Dubofsky (1942- Kansas, Washington, D.C., Colorado)
In 1979, Jean Dubofsky became the first woman justice on the Colorado Supreme Court. She left this position in 1987, to continue as an attorney in private practice, championing equal rights cases.

Claudia Jordan (1953- North Carolina, Colorado)
Claudia Jordan became Colorado's first African-American woman judge in 1994 when she was sworn in as a Denver county court judge.

LAWYERS

Mary Florence Lathrop (1865-1951 Pennsylvania, Colorado)
Mary Lathrop was admitted to practice law in Colorado in 1895. In 1897, Mary Lathrop became the first woman to practice law in Denver and the first U.S. woman member of the American Bar Association, 1917. She was the first woman lawyer admitted to practice before the Colorado U.S. District Court, the U.S. Court of Appeals, and before the U.S. Supreme Court. Before becoming a lawyer, she wrote articles for newspapers and magazines, often traveling by stagecoach. When she became ill with tuberculosis, she came to Denver for her health and then decided to study law at the University of Denver.

Mary Sternberg Thomas (1866-1951 Iowa, Colorado, California)
Many states in the U.S. would not allow women to practice law. The supreme court judges of Colorado thought this was wrong. In 1891, the first two women attorneys in Colorado were Mary Sternberg Thomas and Josephine M. Luthe. It is questionable if Pearl S. King was admitted in 1890. Minnie K. Leibhardt was admitted in 1896.

Norma Comstock MacDougall (1904-1988 Colorado)
In 1965, Norma Comstock became the first woman president of the Denver Bar Association. In 1968, she was elected the first woman officer of the Colorado Bar Association, one of the four vice presidents. In 1932, she was the first woman to place first on the Colorado Bar exam.

Ann Hunt (? -1912, ?, Colorado, ?)
Ann Hunt was the first woman attorney to graduate from a Colorado law school, The University of Denver College of Law, 1894.

Betsy Levin (1935- Maryland, New York, North Carolina, Washington, D.C., Colorado, Washington, D.C.)
Law professor and former research geologist, Betsy Levin, was the first woman dean of a Colorado law school, The University of Colorado School of Law, 1981-1987. She was also the first General Counsel of the U.S. Department of Education, which was established during President Jimmy Carter's administration.

Katherine Tamblyn (1939- Colorado, Kansas, Colorado)
Katherine Tamblyn was the first woman president of the Colorado Bar Association, 1982-1983. She was one of the first women arbitrators for the New York Stock Exchange.

Yvonne Knight (1942- Oklahoma, Kansas, New Mexico, Colorado)
One of the first Native American women to earn a law degree in the U.S. was Yvonne Knight, 1971. She works in Boulder, Colorado with the Native American Rights Fund, a national non-profit law firm. She is a member of the Ponca Tribe of Oklahoma where her father is a tribal leader.

Gale A. Norton (1954- Kansas, Colorado)
In 1991, Gale A. Norton was elected the first woman Attorney General of Colorado.

MUSICIANS AND MUSICAL CAREERS

Miriam Gideon (1907-1996 Colorado, Massachusetts, New York)
Miriam Gideon was a composer of vocal, opera, chamber and orchestral music. She was a specialist in Jewish liturgical music and with her doctorate in composition, taught at the Jewish Theological Seminary in New York.

Lillian (Billie) Stein (1907- Colorado)
In the 1920's and 1930's, Billie Stein toured the U.S. playing her trumpet in an all woman-band. She still performs on the trumpet for organizations.

Louise Sherman (Kansas, New York, California, New York, Italy, France, Colorado)
Louise Sherman is the music director of Opera Colorado and is responsible for all the solo artists and the 150-voice Opera Colorado Chorus. She came to Denver in 1982 for the creation of Opera Colorado, directed by her husband, Nathaniel Merrill. Before that she served with New York's Metropolitan Opera for more than twenty years as their assistant conductor, coaching the world's leading singers. Louise Sherman has worked with more than ninety-five conductors throughout the world.

Jo Ann Falletta (1954- New York)
Jo Ann Falletta was the first woman to be music director of the Denver Chamber Orchestra, 1983-1992. Currently, she is music director of the Virginia Symphony and music director of the Long Beach Symphony in California.

Marin Alsop (1956- New York, Massachusetts, Oregon, Virginia, Colorado)
Besides being the Colorado Symphony Orchestra's first woman music director, a position she has held since 1993, Marin Alsop also conducts symphonies in other U.S. and European cities.

POLITICAL AND GOVERNMENT CAREERS

Since the 1870s, the only issue on which Colorado women were allowed to vote was school board elections. The United States finally granted women the right to vote on all issues in 1920. However, Colorado became the first state to grant women the right to vote, even earlier than the United States, in 1893.

Elected Officials and Politically Active

Eliza Pickrell Routt (1839-1907 ?, Colorado)
Wife of Governor John Routt, Eliza Pickrell Routt was the first woman who registered to vote in Colorado, 1893. She was active in trying to help women gain the right to vote. She was the first woman on the state Board of Agriculture, which oversaw Colorado State University. Her leadership helped create home economics courses.

The first three women to be elected Colorado state legislators in 1894 were **Clara Cressingham**, Denver; **Carrie C. Holly**, a Pueblo lawyer; and **Frances S. Klock**, Denver.

Martha Bushnell Conine (?-1910 New York, Colorado)
Martha Bushnell Conine of Denver was the fourth woman elected to the Colorado legislature, 1896-1899. She worked for reforms to help women and children.

Ione T. Hanna (1837-1924 ?, Colorado)
In 1893, Ione Hanna was the first woman elected to a public office in Denver. She served on the Denver School Board.

Katherine G. Patterson (1839-1902 ?, Colorado)
Katherine Patterson was president of the Colorado Equal Suffrage Association, working to gain the vote for women. Wife of Colorado's first U.S. representative who later became a senator, she helped organize The Denver Orphans Home, the YMCA and the Women's Club.

Owl Woman (18? -? Colorado)
Knowledgeable in several languages, Owl Woman, a Native American, was able to help Hispanic, Native American and Anglo Americans speak with each other. She was married to Charles Bent, working with him in his fur trading business at Bent's fort.

Olive C. Butler (1841-1915 Massachusetts, Colorado)
Olive Butler was one of Colorado's first women legislators, representing Arapahoe County from 1897-1900. She was active in helping women achieve the right to vote.

Helen Ring Robinson (?-1923 Maine, Rhode Island, Colorado)
Helen Robinson, representing Denver, was the first woman elected to the Colorado Senate in 1913. She was interested in women's equality and introduced a bill stating that women should sit on juries. The bill did not pass. She had been a teacher, newspaper editorial writer and lecturer and was invited by Henry Ford to Europe, speaking for peace.

Alice M. Ruble (1849 or 1852-1906 Vermont, Kansas, Colorado)
Alice Ruble was one of Colorado's first women legislators, elected 1903, Denver.

Sarah Platt Decker (1856-1912   Vermont, Colorado)
Sara Platt Decker was a leader in helping Colorado women gain the right to vote. She became the national president of the General Federation of Women's Clubs and was invited to work on the first White House Conference on Child Welfare. Platt Park in south Denver and the Decker branch library were named for her.

Mary C. Craig Bradford (1862-1938   New York, Colorado)
In 1913, Mary C. Craig Bradford was one of the first women nominated for a constitutional elective office in the U.S as superintendent of Public Instruction for Denver. It was an office she held for six terms. She helped Colorado achieve the vote for women, later helping twelve other states. In 1901 she was elected president of the National Woman's Suffrage Association.

Agnes L. Riddle (1865-1930 Germany, Missouri, Colorado)
As a Colorado state representative and senator for Adams, Arapahoe, and Elbert counties from 1911-1920, Agnes Riddle fought and won new dairy and farm inspection laws for the farming people she represented. She helped pass amendments for an eight-hour work day, minimum wage laws and child welfare.

Mabel Cory Costigan (1873-1951 Wisconsin, Colorado, Washington, D.C., Colorado)
In 1928, Mabel Cory Costigan, wife of Senator Edward Costigan, founded the Colorado League of Women Voters.

Nettie Schwer Freed (c.1881-1979 Ohio, Colorado, Utah, Colorado)
In 1946, Nettie Schwer Freed of Pueblo, Colorado, became the first Colorado Commissioner of Education. Prior to that she had been appointed Pueblo County Superintendent of Schools. She helped reform rural education.

Elizabeth Eyre Pellet (1887-1976 Connecticut, New York, Colorado)
Elizabeth Eyre Pellet was the first woman majority leader in the State legislature, serving in the Colorado House of Representatives from 1940-1942, 1948-1964. She sponsored bills creating the division of children and youth and laws which provided education for mentally slower children. When her husband became ill, she managed several of their mines and often worked in the mines.

Eudocia Bell Smith (1887-1977   Texas, Colorado)
In 1936, Eudochia Bell Smith was elected to the House of Representatives and in 1940 to the Colorado Senate. She was re-elected in 1944, and resigned in 1946 when U.S. President Truman gave her a national apppointment.

Mamie Doud Eisenhower (1896-1979   Iowa, Colorado, Texas, Georgia, Panama, Colorado, Kansas, Georgia, France, Washington, D.C., The Phillipines, Washington, D.C., Pennsylvania, Washington, D.C.)
From 1953 to 1961, the Summer White House of U.S. President Dwight D. Eisenhower, was in Denver at 750 Lafayette Street. His wife, Mamie Doud Eisenhower had lived in this home since she was ten years old. As the First Lady of the U.S., Mamie was a gracious hostess to people from all over the world.

Golda Meir (1898-1978   Ukraine, Wisconsin, Colorado, Israel)
Because her parents did not want Golda to continue her high school education, she ran away from home. From 1913 to 1915 she lived in her sister and brother-in-law's home, 1606 Julian Street, in Denver. Family dinner table discussions awakened Golda Meir's awareness of the need for a homeland for Jewish people in Palestine. In 1921, she settled in Palestine, which became Israel. She held many high government positions before becoming the first woman prime minister of Israel, 1969-1974. In 1989, the home in which Golda Meir had lived in Denver was moved to the Auraria campus and is now a state historical landmark and musuem.

Virginia Neal Blue (1910-1970   Colorado)
In 1966, Virginia Neal Blue was the first woman to be elected to a high Colorado office, State Treasurer of Colorado. She had been named Denver Realtor of the Year 1964, was a regent of the University of Colorado and was chairperson of the Colorado Commission on the Status of Women.

Ruth Stockton (1916-1990   New Jersey, Colorado)
Representing Lakewood, Colorado, Ruth Stockton served in the Colorado legislature longer than any other woman: 1961-1964 in the House and 1965-1984 in the Senate. To honor Ruth Stockton, her portrait in a stained glass window was created for Denver's Capitol. It is located near the Senate chambers.

Freda Poundstone (California, Phillipine Islands, Japan, Colorado)
Denver had the right to add land to its boundaries without the people being able to vote on this issue. Freda Poundstone thought this unfair and in 1974 lead the state-wide drive to give people the right to vote on Denver's land boundaries. This became the Poundstone Amendment to the Colorado Constitution. In 1988, Adams County, a suburb, did allow Denver to add 53 square miles for the new Denver International Airport. Freda Poundstone was the first woman mayor of Greenwood Village, elected in 1985.

Arie Taylor (1927- Ohio, Colorado)
The grandaughter of a slave, Arie Taylor became the first black woman state legislator in Colorado, 1972-1984. In 1972, a woman in Colorado could not buy a home in her own name and could not borrow money from a bank. Arie Taylor sponsored bills which became laws changing this. She helped protect the civil rights of Colorado's women.

Swanee Hunt (1950- Texas, Germany, Colorado/Massachusetts)
Swanee Hunt is a philanthropist and a social activist who was appointed U.S. Ambassador to Austria by President Clinton in 1993. She holds advanced degrees in religion and psychology, a doctorate in theology, and speaks three languages. As ambassador, she wrote a column for the *Rocky Mountain News* describing her experiences. Swanee Hunt uses her inherited wealth to support organizations dedicated to helping others.

Mary Estill Buchanan (1934- California, Kentucky, Ohio, New York, New Jersey, Florida, Massachusetts, Connecticut, Colorado)

Mary Estill Buchanan was the first woman Secretary of State of Colorado. Mary's great-grandmother, Missouri Powell Probst, a mail-order bride who came to Colorado in 1874, wrote articles protesting women's limited rights. She would have been proud of her great-granddaughter! Today, Mary Estill Buchanan is writing and speaking about values for better end-of-life medical treatments.

Madeleine Albright (1937- Czechoslovakia, England, Switzerland, Colorado, Massachusetts, Illinois, New York, Washington, D.C.)

In 1996, Madeleine Albright became the first woman to be U.S. Secretary of State. Her family had moved to Colorado when her father, a diplomat, became a professor at the University of Denver in 1949. She was the top student at Kent School for Girls where she founded and chaired the International Relations Club. She lived in Colorado until going to Wellesley College.

Cathy Donohue (1939- Illinois, Missouri, Wyoming, Colorado)

Cathy Donohue was the first woman elected president of the Denver City Council, 1982. She was also the first person ever elected two terms in a row, 1989 to 1991. Cathy Donohue is the first woman director of the Mayor's Office of Regulatory Reform.

Nancy Dick (before 1940's- Michigan, Ohio, Iowa, Oklahoma, Colorado)

Nancy Dick was the first woman Lieutenant Governor of Colorado, serving from 1979 to 1987. After leaving office, she started her own successful mergers and acquisitions company.

Gail Schoettler (1943- California, Colorado)

Gail Schoettler is the first woman to be both Colorado's Lieutenant Governor (elected in 1994) and State Treasurer (from 1987 to 1994.) She serves as chairperson of the Colorado Commission of Indian Affairs and was president of the Douglas County Board of Education. Gail Schoettler served as co-chair of the 1997 "Summit of the Eight" in Denver, an importaant gathering of eight world leaders. She was one of the organizers of the Women's Bank and a founder of Denver's Children's Museum, serving as its board president for ten years. In 1997, Gail Schoettler is making plans to run for the position of Colorado's governor. If she wins, the next printing of this book will be revised!

Polly Baca (1943- Colorado)

Polly Baca was the first minority woman to be elected to the Colorado Senate, 1978. (Please see more in business.)

Cathy Reynolds (1944- Missouri, Colorado)

In 1979, Cathy Reynolds became the first woman president of the Denver City Council, finishing another president's term. She was elected president of the City Council in 1984 and again in 1996.

Gale A. Norton (1954- Kansas, Colorado)

Since 1991, Gale A. Norton has been the first woman Attorney General of Colorado.

SOME OF THE FIRST WOMEN MAYORS OF SELECTED COLORADO CITIES

Grover	**Elizabeth Lawer** became mayor in 1929 supported by an all woman town board, called the "Petticoat government."
Manitou Springs	**Mabel Willie** became mayor in 1953.
Walsenburg	**Mrs. Leo Stacy** became mayor in 1960.
Akron	**Myrtle M. Schaible** became mayor in 1960.
Pueblo	**Georgia Farabaugh** became mayor in 1963.
Arvada	**Ann Jackson** became mayor in 1963.
Las Animas	**Kelly Ann Long** became mayor in 1966.
Deer Trail	**Wanda Jolly** became mayor in 1966.
Telluride	**Bettye C. McPhee** became acting mayor in 1968.
Aspen	**Eve Homeyer** became mayor in 1970.
Fort Collins	**Mable Preble** became mayor in 1973.
Englewood	**Judy Henning** became mayor in 1974.
Fairplay	**Ada Evans**, an African-American, became mayor in 1974.
Boulder	**Ruth Correll** served as mayor from 1977 to 1987.
Thornton	**Margaret Carpenter** became mayor in 1979. She was re-elected five times, her current term expiring in 1999. She is chairperson of the board of the E-470 Public Highway Authority and president of the Colorado Municipal League. In 1997 she became chair of the Denver Regional Council of Governments.
Glenwood Springs	**Meredith Flinn** became city manager in 1980.
Littleton	**Linda Shaw** became mayor in 1983
Longmont	**Leona Stoecker** became mayor in 1993.
Colorado Springs	**Mary Lou Makepeace** became mayor in 1997.

GOVERNMENT CAREERS

Mary Parker Converse   (1872-1961   Massachusetts, Colorado)

Mary Parker Converse was the first woman to be made a captain in the U.S. Merchant Marines. She trained more than 2,500 enlisted men. In addition, she helped change Colorado's penal program and wrote two books, one for children.

Helen Louise White Peterson   (1915-   South Dakota, Colorado, Washington, D.C., Colorado,?)

Attorney and Oglala Sioux Native American, Helen Peterson, was the first director of the Denver Commission on Human Relations, 1948-1953. Moving to Washington, D.C., she became executive director of the National Congress of American Indians. In 1972, Helen Peterson began the first Bureau of Indian Affairs Intergovernmental Relations office in Denver.

Oleta L. Crain   (before 1920's-   Oklahoma, Iowa, Nebraska, Ohio, Massachusetts, Alaska, Germany, New York, England, Washington, D.C., Massachusetts, Colorado)

In 1942, Oleta Crain was the first African-American woman in the Rocky Mountain area to enlist in the Women's Army Auxilliary in Denver. She now is the Regional Administrator for the U.S. Department of Labor Women's Bureau.

Barbara Sudler Hornby   (1925-   Hawaii, Orient, Phillipines, Europe, Washington, D.C., Colorado)

Barbara Sudler Hornby was the first woman to be Colorado's Historic Preservation Officer, 1983 to 1991 and is a member of the Denver Landmark Preservation Commission. The Colorado Historical Society was founded in 1879. One hundred years later she became the first woman president of the Colorado Historical Society. She was a founder of the Women's Bank in Denver.

Wilma Webb   (1943-   Colorado)

In 1997, Wilma Webb became both the first woman and first African-American U.S. Labor Department's regional representative for Region 8, which includes Colorado, Montana, North Dakota, South Dakota, Utah, and Wyoming. Since 1991, she has been an active first lady for the City and County of Denver as the wife of Denver's Mayor, Wellington Webb. As a state representative in the Colorado General Assembly from 1980 to to 1993, she sponsored and carried forty-four bills. In 1983, Wilma Webb was the chief sponsor of the bill providing for the holiday observance of Dr. Martin Luther King Jr.'s birthday in Colorado.

Carol Mutter   (1945-   Colorado, Virginia, California, Virginia, California, Virginia, Japan, Virginia, Rhode Island, Kansas, Colorado, Japan, Virginia, Japan, Virginia, Japan, Virginia, Washington, D.C.)

Carol Mutter of Eaton, Colorado, is a three-star general and the highest ranking woman in the United States Marine Corps. In 1996, Carol Mutter was appointed a Lieutenant General.

Meg Porfido   (1957-   New Jersey, Washington, D.C., Colorado)

Since 1994, attorney Meg Porfido has been the first woman chief of staff for a governor of the State of Colorado, Governor Roy Romer.

PUBLISHERS, WRITERS, JOURNALISTS

PUBLISHERS

Caroline Nichols Churchill   (1843-1926   Canada, Colorado)

In 1879, Caroline Nichols Churchill began Denver's first women's rights newspaper, distributing it throughout the West.

Anna C. Petteys   (1892-1970   Iowa, Colorado)

In northeastern Colorado, Anna C. Petteys was the publisher of *The Sterling Journal Advocate*. She wrote a daily column, a book, and gave lectures about the United Nations, an organization just being formed. Anna Petteys was one of the organizers of the National Association of State School Boards, and was elected its first president and board chair. She helped develop a strong junior college program in Colorado.

Ann Thompson   (1920-   Iowa, Wyoming, Colorado)

Ann Thompson was the first woman elected to the Colorado Journalism Hall of Fame. She edited and published the *Colorado Business Woman*, edited *Tusk Talk*, a newsletter for Colorado's Republican women and publishes the *Rocky Ford Daily Gazette* with her husband. In addition, politically, she has served two terms as state representative from Crowley and Otero counties, 1957-1961.

Miriam Harris Goldberg   (Colorado)

Since 1972, Miriam Harris Goldberg has been editor and publisher of *The Intermountain Jewish News*. Her family has owned this newspaper since 1943, and Miriam Harris Goldberg has been on staff since 1965. At present, three generations of journalists in her family actively participate in the publication.

Alice Borodkin   (1933-   New York, Colorado)

In 1996, Alice Borodkin founded and became the publisher of the *Women's Business Chronicles*, a business newspaper for women.

Wanda M. Padilla   (before 1950's- Illinois, Colorado)

Wanda M. Padilla is one of the founders and the first woman publisher of *La Voz de Colorado* (The Voice of Colorado.) This is Colorado's oldest weekly Hispanic newspaper, founded in 1974.

Terry Vitale   (1945-   New Jersey, Colorado, Minnesota, California, Colorado)

Terry Vitale is the founder and publisher of *Colorado Expressions*, an upscale, lifestyle magazine.

Maurene Regan Smith   (1959-   Kansas, Texas, Colorado, Illinois, Colorado)

Maurene Regan Smith is the president of American Parent Communications, which publishes *Colorado Parent* magazine, *Northern Colorado Parent* and *Southern Colorado Parent*. She also is owner of a Texas business magazine. Prior to this, for eight years, she was the first woman publisher and president of the forty-year old *Denver Business Journal*, a weekly business newspaper.

WRITERS, JOURNALISTS

Grace Greenwood (1823-1904 New York, Pennsylvania, Ohio, New York)
Washington Post newspaper columnist, lecturer, and author of fourteen books, Grace Greenwood highly praised Colorado in her writing while spending summers in Colorado Springs beginning in the 1870's.

Susan Shelby Magoffin (1828-1852 Kentucky, Colorado, New Mexico Mexico, Missouri)
Susan Shelby Magoffin, the first white woman to travel along the Sante Fe Trail, 1846, kept a diary of her prairie experiences using vivid descriptions.

Isabella Bishop Bird (1831-1904 England)
Isabella Bird, a world traveler, visited Colorado in the summer of 1873. She climbed the 14,256 foot Long's Peak mountain near Estes Park and described her experiences in letters to her sister in England. The letters became a book, *A Lady's Life in the Rocky Mountains*, now in its 13th printing.

Mary Hallock Foote (1847-1938 New York, Colorado, Idaho, Mexico, Massachusetts)
Mary Hallock Foote wrote and illustrated articles and novels about Leadville, Colorado. She increased awareness that newcomers to the West were environmentally careless about the areas around mining towns after they made their fortunes.

Alice Polk Hill (1854-1921 ?, Colorado)
Poet and author of *Tales of the Colorado Pioneers*, Alice Polk Hill was appointed Colorado's first Poet Laureate by Governor Shoup in 1919. Alice Polk Hill was the sole woman on a committee to write the charter for the City and County of Denver.

Leonel Ross Campbell (Polly Pry) (1857-1938 Mississippi, Missouri, Mexico, New York, Colorado)
After writing for a New York newspaper, Leonel Ross Campbell joined the staff of *The Denver Post*. She took the name Polly Pry and wrote feature stories, traveling to all parts of the world.

Katherine Lee Bates (1859-1929 Massachusetts, England, Massachusetts)
In 1893, Katherine Lee Bates, Wellesley College professor of English, was teaching a summer school class at Colorado College in Colorado Springs. She was so inspired by Colorado's mountain views, especially Pikes Peak, that she wrote the poem *America The Beautiful*. It was written in its final form in 1904.

Minnie J. Reynolds (1865-1936 ?, Colorado, New York, New Jersey)
Rocky Mountain News Society Editor Minnie J. Reynolds founded The Denver Women's Press Club in 1898. Active in helping women gain the right to vote, she influenced many of Colorado's newspapers to support this cause. In New York, she wrote novels and magazine articles.

Anne Parrish (1888-1957 Colorado, Connecticut)
Colorado Springs author, Anne Parrish, wrote popular novels.

Elinor Bluemel (1894-1975 Kansas, Colorado)
Elinor Bluemel wrote biographies of Coloradans: Emily Griffith, Dr. Florence Sabin, Dr. Charles Sidney Bluemel, her husband, and a book tracing one hundred years of Colorado women. With her husband, she owned and managed Mount Airy Sanitorium. She was president of the Denver Women's Press Club, the Colorado Authors' League and a director of the Denver Orphans' Home.

Agnes Wright Spring (1894-1988 Colorado, Wyoming, Colorado)
Agnes Wright Spring, a civil engineer, became State Historian both for Colorado and Wyoming. In addition, she wrote twenty books, articles and a play.

Lenora Mattingly Weber (1895-1971 Missouri, Colorado)
Lenora Mattingly Weber wrote children's books. Her most popular were the series involving a Colorado girl, Beanie Malone.

Caroline Bancroft (1900-1985 Colorado)
Caroline Bancroft was the author of many books about the history and women of Colorado such as Augusta Tabor, Baby Doe, and Molly Brown. She may have gained her interest in history from her grandfather, Dr. Frederick Bancroft, president of the State Historical Society for seventeen years. Both the Denver Public Library and the Colorado Historical Society give an annual Caroline Bancroft History Award. The library's award is for the best non-fiction book about the American West; the historical society's award is for the best state history project..

Mary Coyle Chase (1907-1981 Colorado)
Playwright Mary Coyle Chase's most famous play was *Harvey* which won the 1945 Pulitzer Prize. She was also a reporter for the *Rocky Mountain News*, a children's book author and taught writing at the University of Denver.

Chris Petteys (1927- Colorado)
Chris Petteys of Sterling, Colorado, researched, compiled and wrote the amazing 851 page *Dictionary of Women Artists*, an international dictionary of women artists born before 1900. She included more than 21,000 women painters, sculptors, printmakers and illustrators. Chris Petteys also served on the Board of Trustees at the Denver Art Museum, the state board of the Colorado Council of the Arts and Humanities and is a founding member of the National Museum of Women in the Arts, Washington, D.C., serving on the museum's National Advisory Board.

Dottie Lamm (1937- New York, California, Colorado)
Dottie Lamm is an author, political activist, motivational speaker, free-lance writer and was a newspaper columnist for seventeen years for *The Denver Post*. She has traveled world-wide in her position as Presidential Delegate to the United Nations Commission on the Status of Women. She traveled throughout Colorado during the years when her husband, Richard Lamm, was Colorado's Governor, 1975-1987. In 1997, she is a candidate for the U.S. Senate.

Sandra Dallas (1939- Washington, D.C., Colorado, Utah, Colorado)
Sandra Dallas has helped record the past in the non-fiction books she has written, most of which describe Colorado and Denver's history. In addition, she has written three novels, is a book reviewer and writes articles for *Business Week* magazine.

Joanne Dodds   (1944-   California, Colorado)
Author of books describing Pueblo, Colorado's history, Joanne Dodds is also the assistant director of the Pueblo Library District.

Clarissa Pinkola Estés   (1943-   Michigan, Colorado, Wyoming)
Clarissa Pinkola Estés was born to Mexican/Indian parents and adopted by Hungarian parents. She felt lucky to be an adoptee bridging two cultures. As a doctor in psychology, she treats patients in Colorado and Wyoming and has written articles and poems. In her successful book *Women Who Run with the Wolves*, she states that women must trust their powerful instincts. Clarissa Pinkola Estés has been an artist-in-residence for the state of Colorado.

Susan Heitler   (1945-   Illinois, Massachusetts, Colorado)
Ph.D. clinical psychologist Susan Heitler, has written three books and created audio tapes which help people feel good about themselves and enjoy positive relationships with others.

Joanne Greenberg   (1932-   New York, Colorado)
Joanne Greenberg is an author whose best-known book is *I Never Promised You A Rose Garden*. She is also a professor of anthropology at the Colorado School of Mines teaching engineers to better understand other cultures.

Audrey Friedman Marcus   (1931-   New York, New Jersey, Connecticut, Colorado)
With Rabbi Raymond Zwerin of Denver, Audrey Friedman Marcus writes and publishes Jewish educational materials and books which are used throughout the world. Their writings have gender neutral language and deal with subjects not usually found in school books: death, divorce, conversion, and relationships.

Sybil Downing   (1930-   Colorado, Massachusetts, New York, Connecticut, Illinois, Colorado)
Boulder author Sybil Downing was the first president, 1994-1996, and co-founder of Women Writing the West, an organization drawing attention to women's contributions. Her great-grandmother, Kate Patterson, fought strongly for women's right to vote in Colorado in the 1870's. Sybil Downing and co-author Jane Valentine Barker wrote thirteen books for children and young adults and three other works. Sybil Downing presided over the Boulder Valley Board of Education, 1967-1974, and also chaired the Colorado State Board of Education, 1984-1995.

Sherri Vasquez   (1963-   Colorado, Spain, Colorado)
Sherri Vasquez is president of the Colorado Hispanic Media Association. She writes feature articles and a column about Hispanic issues for the *Rocky Mountain News* and began "Las Noticias," an award-winning bilingual weekly section. Sherri Vasquez was press secretary for Governor Roy Romer's 1990 re-election campaign and researched for the *Spanish News Wire Service* and *The New York Times* bureau in Madrid in 1986.

SCIENCE CAREERS/MEDICINE

From 1860 to 1864, two medical societies were founded in Colorado with only male physicians. The few women physicians who applied were refused membership until 1877. In 1881, Colorado began to grant medical licenses. By 1894, Colorado's four medical schools were accepting women students.

Dr. Alida Avery   (1833-? New York, Colorado)
Dr. Alida Avery, a graduate of the New England Female Medical College in Boston, arrived in Denver in the early 1870's and is thought to be the first woman to practice medicine in Colorado. She was elected vice president of the Women's Suffrage Association, 1876.

Dr. Eleanor M. Lawney   (1851-1922 Massachusetts, Colorado)
Dr. Eleanor Lawney attended the Women's Medical College of Philadelphia and for health reasons moved to Denver continuing her medical studies. In 1887, she was the first woman to graduate as a physician from the University of Denver's College of Medicine, which became the University of Colorado Health Sciences Center. She founded and was president of the Fowler Mission, which became the Denver Visiting Nurse Association. Dr. Eleanor Lawney directed the Globeville Day Nursery, became president of the State Board of Charities and Corrections in 1903, was on the staff of Denver Children's Hospital, and wrote many medical articles.

Dr. Edith Root   (? -1908 ? Illinois, Colorado)
A graduate of the Women's Medical College of Chicago in 1875, she moved to Arapahoe County. In 1881, the first year Colorado began granting medical licenses, Dr. Edith Root was the first woman granted a medical license in Colorado, Number 89.

Dr. Mary Elizabeth Bates   (1861-1954 Wisconsin, Colorado)
Dr. Mary Elizabeth Bates arrived in Denver in 1891, practiced medicine, and was a leader in helping women achieve the vote. She was also responsible for several Colorado laws which protected animals and the establishment of the Mary Elizabeth Bates Foundation for the care of animals.

Louie Croft Boyd   (1871-1951 New York, Colorado)
Louie Croft Boyd helped organize the Colorado State Nurses' Association and worked to have a law which licensed nurses. In 1905, she became Colorado's first licensed nurse. She was the superintendent of nursing in several Colorado hospitals, taught at universities and wrote several books.

Dr. Susan Anderson   (1870-1960 Indiana, Colorado)
Known as "Doc Susie," Dr. Susan Anderson was a physician in Cripple Creek during the gold rush. In 1907, she moved to Fraser, Colorado, where she was the only doctor for nearly fifty years.

Dr. Margaret Ethel Fraser   (1871-1962, Canada, Massachusetts, Colorado)

Because the U.S. refused her services as a physician during World War I, Dr. Margaret Ethel Fraser served with the French army. She also loved the mountains, which led her to be one of the original members of the Colorado Mountain Club, 1912.

Dr. Ella Mead   (1874-1961 New York, Colorado)

A graduate of the University of Denver Medical School, Dr. Ella Mead practiced for over fifty-four years in Greeley, Colorado. She helped create child guidance clinics, organized one of the earliest U.S. birth control clinics, and organized the first public health department in Weld County.

Dr. Portia McKnight Lubchenco   (1887-1978 South Carolina, Russia, South Carolina, Colorado)

Dr. Portia McKnight Lubchenco practiced in Russia, and later escaped from the Communists with her husband and children, sometimes eating only birdseed. She returned to her native South Carolina to practice, driving her horse and buggy to see patients. "Dr. Portia" became legendary as a good and caring doctor. She was the first chief of staff at Logan County Hospital. From age eighty to eighty-five, she joined the Denver Clinic, caring for patients in thirteen nursing homes. She received numerous awards including becoming the first woman ever inducted into the South Carolina Hall of Science and Technology.

Hazel Schmoll   (1890-1990 Colorado, New York, Illinois, Colorado)

Hazel Schmoll, Ph.D., was a botanical researcher who was responsible for protecting the blue columbine. Her work and guidance encouraged its selection as Colorado's state flower. In 1924, she created a survey of Colorado's wildflowers.

Dr. Edith Jackson   (1895?-1964? Colorado)

Edith Jackson was a pediatrician and child psychiatrist. She was best known for encouraging the idea of "rooming in," in which newborn babies stay in the same room with their mother, rather than in a separate nursery.

Dr. Henrika Cantwell   (1925- Switzerland, New York, Colorado)

Dr. Henrika Cantwell is an international expert on child neglect and abuse. The pamphlet she wrote, "Standards of Child Neglect," was selected for use by the U.S. Department of Health, Education, and Welfare. In 1975, she began a program of re-parenting, teaching parents to do a better job of caring for their children.

Theo Colborn   (1927- New Jersey, Colorado Washington, D.C.)

Theo Colborn, Ph.D., is a senior scientist with the World Wildlife Fund in Washington, D.C. She co-authored the book *Our Stolen Future*, describing how human-made chemicals can harm the unborn child. Theo Colborn often returns to her home in Paonia, Colorado. Here she first became concerned with the misuse of western water and its possible effects on the health of people.

SCIENCE CAREERS/ENGINEERS, GEOLOGISTS

Joan Gosink   (1941- New York, Massachusetts, Oregon, Virginia, Alaska, Maryland, Colorado)

Joan Gosink, a mechanical engineer, is the first woman director of the Division of Engineering at Colorado School of Mines.

Susan Steele Weir   (1949- Illinois, Colorado)

Susan Steele Weir, a tunnel geologist, is the first Colorado woman and second woman nationally to serve as president of the Association of Engineering Geologists, a national technical organization.

Susan Landon   (1950- Illinois, New York, Colorado, Texas, Colorado)

Susan Landon is the first Colorado woman and second woman nationally to be president of the American Geological Institute. Susan Landon, a petroleum geologist, was also the first woman president of the American Institute of Professional Geologists.

Laurie Mathews   (1952- Germany, many European and U.S. cities, Colorado)

Civil engineer and environmental biologist, Laurie Mathews became the first woman director of the Colorado State Parks, 1991.

Vicki Cowart   (1953- Arizona, Colorado)

In 1993, Vicki Cowart became the first woman State Geologist and director of the Colorado Geological Survey.

SPORTS

BASKETBALL

Ceal Barry   (1955- Kentucky, Ohio, Colorado)

University of Colorado's Women's Basketball coach since 1983, Ceal Barry has lead her team to more winning seasons than any previous coach. In 1996, she was the assistant coach for the gold medal winning U.S. Olympic Women's Basketball Team. Ceal Barry, named Coach-of-the-Year many times, encourages players to achieve their goals in athletic competition and academic achievement while developing positive character traits. Her team has been recognized for their high level of sportsmanship, receiving three Big Eight Sportsmanship trophies.

BICYCLING

Connie Carpenter Phinney   (1957- Wisconsin, Colorado)

1984 was the first year the Women's Road Race, 79 kilometers, was introduced in the Olympics. Connie Carpeter Phinney of Boulder, Colorado, won the gold medal for this cycling event. She was inducted into both the United States Olympic Hall of Fame in 1992 and the Colorado Sports Hall of Fame. With her husband Davis Phinney, she wrote a cycling training book. She is president of Carpenter/Phinney Bike Camp, Inc.

GOLF

Joan Birkland   (1928- Colorado)

Joan Birkland was inducted into the Colorado Golf Hall of Fame in 1977 and into the Colorado Sports Hall of Fame in 1981. She won many state golf and tennis championships, winning the state for both sports in 1962 and 1964. Joan Birkland has been the executive director of Sports Women of Colorado since 1985.

Judy Bell   (1936- Kansas, Colorado)

In 1996, Judy Bell became the first woman president in the 102 years of the U.S. Golf Association. She has won national amateur golf tournaments and played on the U.S. women's international amateur team for the Curtis Cup in 1960 and 1962. Judy Bell was inducted into the Colorado Sports Hall of Fame in 1996. In addition, she is a co-owner of five elegant shops at the Broadmoor Hotel, Colorado Springs, the city in which she lives.

JOCKEY

Anna Lee Aldred   (1921- Colorado, California, Colorado)

In 1983, Anna Lee Aldred became the first woman jockey to be inducted into the National Cowgirl Hall of Fame.

RODEO

Bertha Kaeperneck Blancett   (1883-1979 Ohio, Colorado, California)

Bertha Kaeperneck Blancett was the world champion woman rodeo rider in 1914-1915. She was inducted into the National Cowboy Hall of Fame in 1975.

RUNNING

Essie Garrett   (1947- Texas, Colorado)

Each year Essie Garrett runs long distances for charity. People pledge money for each mile she runs. She circles Denver's Capitol for two days at Thanksgiving for the homeless. In 1996, Essie Garrett ran 1500 miles from Atlanta to Denver for The Childrens's Hospital HIV Aids Program, raising over $63,000. African-American Essie Garrett grew up in poverty and has chosen to have few material possessions, knowing that "richness comes from within."

SKATING

Peggy Fleming   (1948- California, Ohio, California, Colorado, California)

Figure-skater on ice, Peggy Fleming was the only person from the U.S. to win a gold medal at the 1968 Winter Olympics, Grenoble, France. A few years before winning she had moved to Colorado Springs to study with skating coach, Carlo Fassi. She later toured with the Ice Follies and became a television commentator for skating events. She was inducted into the Colorado Sports Hall of Fame in 1970.

SKIING

Louise A. White   (1906- Colorado, Arizona)

In 1983, Louise A. White was inducted into the Colorado Ski Hall of Fame for her excellence in skiing from 1932 through 1940 and for founding the Colorado Skiing Association, the first women's ski association.

Elizabell "Willie" Williams   (1931-1991 Texas, Colorado)

As a nurse at Denver's Children's Hospital, Willie Williams coordinated a skiing program for young patients with amputations. In 1970, the program moved to Winter Park, Colorado, which was the beginning of the National Sports Center for the Disabled (NSCD). Willie Williams' students won many U.S. and international racing awards while raising their self-esteem. Willie Williams was inducted into the Colorado Ski Hall of Fame in 1996.

TENNIS

Phyllis Lockwood   (1914-1981 Colorado)

For eleven years, Phyllis Lockwood won almost every Colorado tennis championship and seven Intermountain crowns, retiring in 1941. Playing on the National Women's AAU basketball team, she was named to the All-American team in 1949. In 1977, Phyllis Lockwood was inducted into the Colorado Sports Hall of Fame. Of all her awards, she most valued the ones given in her name to young people for outstanding sportsmanship.

VOLUNTEER ACTIVISTS

Elizabeth Summer Byers (1834-1920 Ohio, Colorado)

Elizabeth Byers, a pioneer, came to Colorado with her husband, William, founder of Denver's first newspaper, the *Rocky Mountain News*. Elizabeth Summer Byers was a leader in forming organizations such as the Ladies Relief Home Society, the Y.W.C.A., the Women's Club, the Women's Press Club and the E.M. Byers Home for Boys.

Mother Frances Xavier Cabrini (1850-1917 Italy, New York, Colorado, Illinois)

Frances Cabrini founded sixty-seven convents, schools, hospitals and orphanges in the United States, including two schools in Denver, The Catholic Church declared her a saint in 1946. A shrine in her memory was built on Lookout Mountain near Denver.

Ella Strong Denison (1855-1940 Massachusetts, Iowa, Colorado)

As the daughter of the president of the Santa Fe Railroad, Ella knew she had civic responsiblities. In 1880, Ella was a member of the committees which started the Denver Public Library and the Young Women's Christian Association, the YWCA. In 1907 she was president of The Mothers Congress which grew into the Parent-Teacher Association. She became interested in medical research because of her marriage to a doctor and her friendship with Dr. Florence Sabin. Ella Strong Denison generously gave money to medical schools for research and donated a laboratory building to the University of Colorado. She donated money for libraries in California, the library at Fairmount School in Denver and the Charles Denison Memorial Library Building at Colorado General Hospital, today called the University of Colorado Health Sciences Center.

Agnes Reid Tammen (1865-1942 Virginia, Colorado)

Agnes Reid Tammen and her husband, Harry Tammen, co-founder of *The Denver Post*, donated large sums of money to the Denver Children's Hospital and many other organizations which helped youth and needy older people.

Anne Evans (1871-1941 England, Colorado)

Anne Evans came to Colorado because her father was appointed by Abraham Lincoln to be the second territorial governor of Colorado. Anne Evans was a member of the Denver library committee, and helped form the Central City Opera House Association. As a founder of the Denver Art Museum, she encouraged the display of Native American art, donating many works from her own collection.

Mabel Cory Costigan (1873-1951 ?, Colorado)

In 1928, Mabel Cory Costigan, one of Denver's first kindergarten teachers, founded the Colorado League of Women Voters. She was the wife of U.S. Senator Edward Costigan.

Fannie Lorber (1881-1958 Russia, Colorado)

Denver social worker Fannie Lorber, along with her friend Minnie Willens, raised money through donations to open the Denver Sheltering Home for orphans and children of tuberculosis patients. After several years, the home specialized in the care of children with severe asthma and was renamed Jewish National Home for Asthmatic Children, headed by Fannie Lorber. In 1973 the home merged with what today is The National Jewish Medical and Research Center.

Carla Denison Swan (1884-1943 Colorado)

Following the example of her parents, Dr. Charles and Ella Denison, Carla Denison Swan was active in many organizations, including director of the Denver Children's Hospital. She took a post-graduate course in accounting and finance at the University of Denver to better advise the many organizations for which she served on budget and finance committees.

Julia Penrose (1870-1956 Michigan, Colorado)

To help cure the tuberculosis of her first husband, Julia Lewis McMillan moved to a home at 30 West Dale Street, Colorado Springs. In 1919, she donated this home for an art school and exhibition center, the Broadmoor Art Academy. In 1936, she guided the construction of a new building on this same site, renamed the Colorado Springs Fine Arts Center. Julia Penrose married her second husband Spencer Penrose, and encouraged his founding of many Colorado Springs institutions.

Helen Daly Peale (? ? Colorado)

In 1919, Helen Daly Peale became the first president of the Denver Junior League, formed in 1918. The women members raise money and give their time for a variety of worthwhile community causes.

Elizabeth Paepcke (1902-1994 Illinois, Colorado)

Elizabeth Paepcke saw the beauty of Aspen, and convinced her husband Walter to settle there. They both changed Aspen from a ghost town to an international resort, music and art center. The Paepckes began the Aspen Institute for Humanistic Studies, the Aspen Music Festival, the International Design Conference, and with Elizabeth Paepcke's brother, the Aspen Skiing Company.

Polly Grimes (1903- Colorado, New York, Colorado)

Since 1961, Polly Grimes has sponsored The Polly Grimes Town Hall lecture series, bringing stimulating people in the arts, theatre, and education to address the public. Polly Grimes founded the Denver Center for the Performing Arts Guild to help support theatre.

Marion Gottesfeld (1917- New York, Massachusetts, Colorado)

At the University of Denver, Marion Gottesfeld was the first chairperson of the Chancellors Society and founded or co-founded the following for the university: The Women's Library Association, Lamont Music Associates, the Board of Governors, the Humanities Institute, and DUART. Marion Gottesfeld was the first woman on the board of the Urban Renewal Authority serving from 1965 to 1986. She founded Angels Befriending Children (ABC) for the Hospice of Metro Denver, and began COPE, an organization for inner city childrens whose lives are in danger.

Grace Hale Jordan (1918- Colorado, West Indies, West Africa, Korea, Ecuador, Thailand, Colorado)

African-American civil rights activist, Grace Hale Jordan, helped fight prejudice against black people through the Congress on Racial Equlity, CORE, in Denver in the 1940's and continued as an active community volunteer throughout the world.

Katie Stapleton (1919- Missouri, Colorado)

Katie Stapleton founded the Denver Debutante Ball in 1955, which has raised over two million dollars for the Colorado Symphony. She was also the first Denver woman to be chairperson and board vice president of the Denver Community Chest, now Mile High United Way, and board vice president of Washington, D.C.'s National Cathedral. She has been president or director locally and nationally of the Crippled Children's Aid Fund, Inc., Traveler's Aid, National Council of USO, Denver Chapter of Experiment in International Living, Colorado Women's College, and she was founder of American Field Service, Colorado chapter.

Elizabeth Yanish Shwayder (1920's- Missouri, Colorado)

From 1982 to 1989, Elizabeth Yanish Shwayder organized a Denver program to gather used coats and give them to people in need for winter warmth. She likewise began the New York City coat drive, New York Cares. After this highly successful coat campaign was launched, she began Colorado Operation Paperback, collecting used books to be shipped to United States military people stationed in other countries. In 1996, 15,000 pounds of books were shipped free of charge to Bosnia by United Air Cargo, also arranged by her. From 1992 to 1995, she organized Common Cents, a penny drive with money raised going to Samaritan House.

Ethelyn Thatcher Jones Potestio (1934- Colorado)

Since 1967, Ethelyn Thatcher Jones Potestio has been actively involved in Rosemount Museum in Pueblo, Colorado, the home her great-grandparents built. She was the first woman president of Pueblo's United Way, 1976, and first woman chair of the auction of Pueblo's PBS television, KTSC.

Elizabeth Frawley (1935- Oklahoma, Texas, Montana, Borneo, Hong Kong, Texas, Colorado)

Elizabeth Frawley has been president or an officer on many corporate and guild boards, all of which raise money for worthy causes such as The Gathering Place, The Fine Arts Foundation Corporate Board, The Denver Center Alliance, The Denver Art Museum, Kempe Foundation, Multiple Sclerosis Center Guild, and Food Bank of the Rockies.

Pat Kelly (1923- Colorado)

In 1972, Pat Kelly was a co-founder of Pueblo, Colorado's Sangre de Cristo Arts and Conference Center, which today is the largest arts facility in southeast Colorado. She is heading the Historic Arkansas River Project (HARP), bringing a waterway to downtown Pueblo.

Josepha (Jossy) Eyre (1935- The Netherlands, New York, Colorado, West Virginia, Colorado)

Jossy Eyre wanted homeless, poor women to learn skills to become self-sufficient. In 1989, she began The Women's Bean Project helping women earn money by packaging bean soup mixes which are sold in stores.

LaRita Archibald (1931- Nebraska, Kansas, Colorado)

In 1980, LaRita Archibald founded Heartbeat in Colorado Springs, which has become a nationwide support organization for survivors after suicide.

Annette Finesilver (1935- Illinois, Colorado)

In 1979, the first executive director of the "9Health Fair" sponsored by KUSA Television was Annette Finesilver, wife of Judge Sherman Finesilver, retired Chief Judge of the Colorado U.S. District Court, 1983-1995. She is president-elect of the national board of Allegheny University of the Health Sciences Center, formerly the Medical College of Pennsylvania, which was the first medical school in the U.S. to admit women.

Kathy Farley (1936- Colorado)

In Pueblo, Colorado, Kathy Farley was a co-founder of the Sangre de Cristo Arts and Conference Center, now the largest arts facility in southeast Colorado. Kathy Farley is also the first woman elected as chair of the Pueblo Board of County Comissioners.

Nellie Mae Duman (Colorado)

Involved in many civic organizations, Nellie Mae Duman founded the Opera Colorado Guild in 1981 and was its first president, 1981-1983. In 1982 she chaired the first Opera Colorado Ball, chairing this again in 1997 for the 15th anniversary. When the Denver Symphony was having financial problems, several groups merged in 1980 into the Coordinating Council of the Denver Symphony, to save this community treasure. Nellie Mae Duman was the first president. The Denver Symphony died, but the Colorado Symphony was born.

Jessica Marie Luna (1936-1982 ? Colorado)

Active as a community volunteer in Pueblo, Colorado, Jessica Marie Luna later moved to Denver and became one of the founders of Denver's Children's Museum.

Dottie Lamm (1937- New York, California, Colorado)

In 1986, Dottie Lamm was the first president and one of the founders of the Women's Foundation of Colorado, an organization which provides money for programs to help women and girls with employment skills, job opportunities, and financial counseling. (please see more on Dottie Lamm under writers)

Marilyn Van Derbur Atler (1937- Colorado)

Marilyn Van Derbur Atler had the courage to publicly share her own abuse. She has turned personal tragedy into helping others and speaks throughout the U.S. to protect children's rights. In 1958, she represented Colorado and became Miss America.

Barb Halsell (1937- Colorado)

Barb Halsell was the first director of Denver's "Run for the Zoo."

Cynthia Kahn (1939- Connecticut, Ohio, Massachusetts, Colorado)

Cynthia Kahn was one of the founders of Denver's Children's Museum and the first chair of its board.

Juana Maria Bordas (1942- Nicaragua, Florida, Chile, Wisconsin, Colorado)

Juana Maria Bordas was the first Hispanic woman to become a Colorado certified psychiatric social worker. In 1976, together with a group of community women and other professionals, Juana Maria Bordas founded Mi Casa, and was its executive director for ten years. Mi Casa is a self-improvement organization for Hispanic women and teen-age girls, stressing business and career development skills. Juana Maria Bordas was the first president and CEO of the National Hispana Leadership Institute.

Kim Matusunaga (1941- South Korea, Colorado)

Orphan children in Asian countries have very difficult lives. Kim Matusunaga, a social worker, has arranged the adoption of 800 Asian babies for families in Colorado. She counsels adoptive families through her Berthoud, Colorado business, A.A.C. Adoption & Family Network Inc. Kim Matusunaga travels to Korea or China twice a year, often introducing adoptees to their birth families.

Elaine Gantz Berman (1948- New York, Columbia, Colorado, Washington, D.C., Colorado)

Elaine Gantz Berman is a program officer for the Piton Foundation, a private operating foundation which helps to improve the quality of life for low-income people in Denver. Through the Piton Foundation, Elaine was a founder of the Rocky Mountain Adoption Exchange, and helped start the Colorado Children's Campaign. She helped to create the Denver Public School's Family Resource Schools, a national model for family involvement in children's education. As co-chair with Bob Loup, 1991-1995, and as board president of the Robert E. Loup Jewish Community Center, 1995-1997, she oversaw the renovation of the building and the quadrupling of members and programs.

Dianna Kunz (1948- Colorado)

Dianna Kunz is the first woman president and CEO of Volunteers of America of Colorado.

Kathy Carfrae (1961- Texas, Colorado)

Most shelters for homeless people are only open at night. Homeless women often have small children, a problem when arranging job appointments. Because of this, in 1986 social worker Kathy Carfrae co-founded The Gathering Place, a shelter in Denver open during the day. This helps homeless people to look for a job during the day.

RESERVED FOR A FUTURE FIRST

BY A COLORADO WOMAN

RESERVED FOR A FUTURE FIRST

BY A COLORADO WOMAN

BIBLIOGRAPHY

Amole, Gene. "'Dragon Lady' rules over restoration." *Rocky Mountain News, September 25, 1991, p.28.*

Athearn, Robert G. *The Coloradans.* Albequerque, New Mexico: University of New Mexico Press, 1976.

Berke, Arnold. "Preservation Laureates....Dana Crawford" *National Trust, November/December 1995, pp.72,73.*

Bluemel, Elinor. *One Hundred Years of Colorado Women.* Denver, Colorado: n.p., 1973.

Bluemel, Elinor. *The Golden Opportunity. The Story of the Unique Emily Griffith Opportunity School of Denver.* Boulder, Colorado: Johnson Publishing Company, 1965.

Bluemel, Elinor. *The Opportunity School and Emily Griffith Its Founder.* Denver, Colorado: Green Mountain Press, 1970.

Brinkley, John. "Pat Answers. Highs and lows of Congress never got Schroeder down." *Rocky Mountain News, December 8, 1996, pp. 19,21D.*

Bronikowski, Lynn. "Hach Co. heads the list of women-owned firms." *Rocky Mountain News, May 15, 1994, p.90A.*

Brown, Joseph G. *History of Equal Suffrage in Colorado.* Denver, Colorado: News Job Printing Company, 1898.

Bueler, Gladys R. *Colorado's Colorful Characters.* Golden, Colorado: The Smoking Stack Press, 1970.

Burt, Olive. *Ouray The Arrow.* New York: Julian Messmer, 1953.

Casey, Lee. "Pinky Isn't Deluded by Arty Nonsense." *Rocky Mountain News, February, 1948, P.21.*

Collins, Judy. *Trust Your Heart.* Boston: Houghton Mifflin, 1987.

Cooper, Victoria. "Legendary Five Points obstetrician brought 7,000 youngsters into the world." *Rocky Mountain News, February 22, 1991, pp. 67,69.*

DeMund, Mary. *Women Physicians of Colorado.* Denver, Colorado: The Range Press, 1976.

Dier, Caroline Lawrence. *Lady of the Gardens, Mary Elitch Long.* Hollywood: Hollycrofters, Inc. Ltd., 1932.

Eicher, Diane. "She bridged the gap in Papago history." *The Denver Post, September 23, 1979, pp. 6,7.*

Erickson, David L. "Mary Thomas: Colorado's First Woman Lawyer." *The Colorado Lawyer, Vol. 21, No. 4, 1992.*

Fay, Abbot. *Famous Coloradans.* Paonia, Colorado: Mountain Top Books, 1990. Produced with support of the Colorado Endowment for the Humanities, Denver, Colorado, a grantee of the National Endowment for the Humanities.

Fireside, Bryna J. *Is There a Woman in the House or Senate?* Morton Grove, Illinois: Albert Whiteman and Company, 1994.

Furman, Evelyn E. Livingston. *My Search For Augusta Pierce Tabor, Leadville's First Lady.* Denver, Colorado: Quality Press, 1993.

Germer, Fawn. "Graded unfairly. Sexism plays role in charges against Albino, women say." *Rocky Mountain News, April 6, 1994, pp.6D,7D.*

Grant, Billie Arlene, Anderson, Lynn Editor. *Black Women of the West: Success in the Workplace.* U.S.A.: Gamino Printing, 1982.

Gutierrez, Hector. "Alvarado already major league." *Rocky Mountain News, June 17, 1991, p.15.*

Hafen, LeRoy R. *Men and Women of Colorado.* Denver, Colorado, Phoenix, Arizona: Pioneer Publishing Company of Colorado, 1944.

Hall, Frank, for the Rocky Mountain Historical Company. *History of the State of Colorado, Volume II.* Chicago, Illinois: The Blakely Printing Company, 1890.

Hall, Gordon Langley. *The Two Lives of Baby Doe.* Philadelphia: Macrae Smith Company, 1962.

Hamby, Bruce. "For an enjoyable 'Trip,' take a walk to Larimer Square." *The Denver Post, August 27, 1967, p. 23R.*

Handler, Ruth with Jacqueline Shannon. *Dream Doll, The Ruth Handler Story.* Stamford, Connecticut: Long Meadow Press, 1994.

Hanner, Carol. "U.S. anthropologists honor Underhill's work at gathering." *Rocky Mountain News, November 16, 1984, p.23.*

Hosokawa, Bill. *Thunder in the Rockies.* New York: William Morrow and Company, Inc., 1976.

Hunt, Inez. *The Lady in the Golden Dome.* School District No. 11, in the County of El Paso, State of Colorado, 1973.

Hunt, Inez, Draper, Wanetta W. *Colorado's Restless Ghosts.* Denver, Colorado: Sage Books, Alan Swallow, 1960.

(Illegible.) "Queen Chipeta Goes to Join Husband, Chief Ouray, in Happy Hunting Ground." *The Denver Post, August 18, 1924, p. 1,6.*

Inroy, Tricia. "Hanging On: Judith Albino." *The Denver Post Magazine, October 9, 1994, pp.13,14.*

Jackson, Helen Hunt. *Ramona.* New York: Grossett & Dunlap, Publishers. Copyright 1884 by Roberts Brothers and 1912 by Little, Brown, and Company.

James, Numa L., ed. *The Denver Brand Book, Vol. XIII: 1957, The Denver Posse of the Western News.* Boulder, Colorado: Johnson Publishing Company, 1958.

Johnson, William Oscar and Williamson, Nancy P. *"Whatta-Gal" The Babe Didrikson Story.* Boston, Toronto: Little Brown and Company, A Sports Illustrated Book, 1975.

Jones, Rebecca. "100 Women of Influence, State salutes saints, sports, and suffragists." *Rocky Mountain News, November 8, 1993, pp. 3D,5D,9D.*

Karsner, David. *Silver Dollar, The Story of the Tabors.* New York: Covici Friede Publishers, 1932.

Katz, William Loren. *Black People Who Made the Old West.* Trenton, New Jersey: Africa World Press, 1992. First published by Thomas Y. Crowell Company, 1977.

Kemp, Polly. "Early author was a woman for her time. Helen Hunt Jackson challenged the nation." *The Denver Post,* December 28 1985, pp. C1,C4.

Kensler, Tom. "Breathing lessons, Van Dyken conquers asthma." *The Denver Post,* March 10, 1966, pp. 1B,6B.

Kensler, Tom. "Swimmer outcompetes asthma. Van Dyken barely misses bronze medal." *The Denver Post,* July 21, 1996, pp. 1, 16A.

Kerwin, Katie. "Women who shaped a city." *Rocky Mountain News,* November 20, 1992, pp. 91,136.

Lepage, Jane Weiner. *Women Composers, Conductors, and Musicians of the Twentieth Century. Selected Biographies.* Metuchen, New Jersey and London: The Scarecrow Press, Inc., 1980.

Marranzino, Pasquale. "Frances Wayne Takes Editorship." *Rocky Mountain News,* February 26, 1948, p. 6.

McNair, Doug and McNair Wallace Yvonne. *Colorado Hispanic Leadership Profiles 1991-1992.* Denver, Colorado: Western Images Publications, Inc., 1991.

Meir, Menahem. *My Mother Golda Meir, A Son's Evocation of Life with Golda Meir.* New York: Arbor House, 1983.

Melrose, Frances. "Study of Papagos is fondly recalled." *Rocky Mountain News,* January 23, 1977, pp. 8,54.

Monnett, John H. and McCarthy, Michael. *Colorado Profiles: men and women who shaped the Centennial State.* Evergreen, Colorado: Cordillera Press, Inc., 1987.

Neyman, Gayle and Gallione, Meghan. "The Unvanquished." *Rocky Mountain News.* March 19, 1993, pp. 68,70.

Nicholson, Kieran. "Albino Accepts California Post." *The Denver Post,* December 21, 1996, pp.1B,3B.

Noel, Thomas J. *Denver's Larimer Street, Main Street, Skid Row and Urban Renaissance.* Denver: Historic Denver, Inc., 1981.

O'Neill, Lois Decker, ed. *Women's Book of World Records and Achievements.* Garden City, New York: Anchor Press/Doubleday, 1979.

Ortiz, Alfonso, volume ed., Sturtevant, William C. general ed. *Handbook of North American Indians, Southwest, Volume 10.* Washington, D.C.: Smithsonian Institution, 1983.

Propst, Nell Brown. *Those Strenuous Dames of the Colorado Prairie.* Boulder, Colorado: Pruett Publishing Company, 1982.

Ray, Grace Ernestine. *Wily Women of the West.* San Antonio, Texas: The Naylor Company, 1972.

Romano, Michael. "'I'm Still Learning,' Albino Says." *Rocky Mountain News,* April 17, 1991, pp.6,17.

Romano, Michael. "CU Vice-President Gets Top Post." *Rocky Mountain News,* April 16, 1991, pp.8,20.

Romano, Michael. "Defiant Albino vows not to quit." *Rocky Mountain News,* January 15, 1994, p.4A.

Scheader, Catherine. *Contributions of Women Musicians.* Minneapolis, Minnesota: Dillon Press, Inc., 1985.

Schlosser, Elizabeth. *Modern Art in Denver, 1919-1960, Eleven Denver Artists.* Denver, Colorado: Ocean View Books, 1993.

Schlosser, Elizabeth. *Modern Sculptures in Denver, 1919-1960.* Denver, Colorado: Ocean View Books, 1995.

Seawell, Donald. "To Helen With Love." *Applause Program Magazine,* 1991, p. 7.

Seipel, Tracy. "CU's Newest Chief Thirsts for Challenge." *The Denver Post,* August 12, 1991, pp.1B,3B.

Shumate-Schnellmann, Sue-Ann, Editor. *Colorado Women's History, A Multicultural Treasury.* Denver, Colorado: Colorado Committee for Women's History, 1985.

Sinisi, Sebastian J.. "Albino turns back foes at C.U." *The Denver Post,* January 15, 1994, pp. 1A,17A.

Sinisi, Sebastian J. and Mary George. "Regents stand by Albino." *The Denver Post,* January 21, 1994, pp. 1A,6A,7A.

Sleeth, Peter. "New CU president driven, poised to succeed." *The Denver Post,* April 21, 1991, p.10A.

Sprague, Marshall. *Newport in the Rockies, The Life and Good Times of Colorado Springs.* Chicago, Illinois, Athens, Ohio: Sage Books, Swallow Press, The Ohio University Press, 1961.

Telgen, Diane and Kamp, Jim, Editors. *Notable Hispanic American Women.* Detroit, Washington, D.C., London: Gale Research Inc. 1993.

Trenton, Patricia and D'Andrea, Jeanne. *Independent Spirits, Women Painters of the American West 1890-1945.* Berkeley, Los Angeles, London: Autry Museum of Western Heritage in association with the University of California Press, 1995.

(Unknown) "Helen Hunt Jackson is legendary character. *Colorado Springs Gazette Telegraph,* May 23, 1965, p. 4AA.

Uchill, Ida Libert. *Pioneers, Peddlers, and Tsadikim.* Denver, Colorado: Sage Books, 1957.

Von Ende, Zoe. "Frances Wayne, Star Reporter." *The Denver Post,* February 6, 1972, p. 8,9.

Wharton, J.E. *The City of Denver.* Denver, Colorado: Byers and Dailey Printers, 1866.

Whitacre, Christine. *Molly Brown, Denver's Unsinkable Lady.* Denver, Colorado: Historic Denver, Inc., 1984.

Wilcox, Rhoda D. "Helen Hunt Jackson outstanding early resident." *Colorado Springs Gazette,* February 31, 1961.

Zaharias, Babe Didrikson as told to Harry Paxton. *This Life I've Led, My Autobiography.* New York: A. S. Barnes and Company, Inc., 1955.

Additional books by Vivian Sheldon Epstein
available by ordering from
your local bookstore, wholesale distributor or
VSE Publisher, 212 South Dexter Street, Denver, Colorado 80246

A Common thread among all these books is the elimination of prejudice and the growth of the individual through knowledge that the world is open to us with many possibilities. Role models of the past are depicted to inspire young people. The author believes that changes in societal attitudes can best be created by instilling positive ideas within young people.

HISTORY OF WOMEN IN SCIENCE FOR YOUNG PEOPLE
A topic never before approached for ages 9-14. Exciting and challenging lives of women scientists encourages girls to become involved in science. Approved and applauded by educators, librarians, and scientists in many fields. The American Association for the Advancement of Science called it one of the best science books for young people since 1992. National Science Teachers Association..."charming portraits...written carefully...excellent resource" (September 1994)
Soft Cover: $7.95   ISBN 0-9601002-7-X;   Hard Cover: $14.95   ISBN 0-9601002-8-8

HISTORY OF WOMEN ARTISTS FOR CHILDREN
First book ever written for young people ages 5 to 12 telling women's story as artists from the 1500's to the present... Beautiful museum color reproductions... Booklist..."worthwhile and profusely illustrated"... (March 88) National Art Education Association..."very attractive, interesting and information packed" (October 88)... Chosen by Choices as one of the best books of 1987... 32 pages, 8"x12", 16 in full vibrant color.
Soft Cover: $6.95   ISBN 0-9601002-5-3;   Hard Cover: $13.95   ISBN 0-9601002-6-1

HISTORY OF WOMEN FOR CHILDREN
The Council on Interracial Books for Children called this book "EXTRAORDINARY." For the first time, a chronological story of the history of women for children is told; ages 5 to 12. Highlighted as one of five of the best 600 children's books by *A Guide to Non-Sexist Children's Books, Vol. II: 1976-1985*... 32 pages, 8"x12", 8 in full vibrant color.
Soft Cover: $6.95   ISBN 0-9601002-3-7;   Hard Cover: $13.95   ISBN 0-9601002-4-5

THE ABCS OF WHAT A GIRL CAN BE
Delightful alphabet book describing the wide range of professions available to women today, all with non-sexist job titles. Attractive color drawing accompany rhyming text. 32 pages, 8"x12", 8 in full vibrant color.   Soft Cover: $6.95   ISBN 0-9601002-2-9

Please add $1.50 postage; Colorado residents add sales tax.

COMMENTS ABOUT HISTORY OF COLORADO'S WOMEN FOR YOUNG PEOPLE

"The remarkable accomplishments of women in the founding and development of our state have been too long overlooked and too little appreciated. Vivian Sheldon Epstein makes a significant contribution to our appreciation of these outstanding Coloradans, who so clearly demonstrated that society can ill afford to ignore or artificially limit the brain power, talent and energy of half its citizens."

Gail S. Schoettler, Lieutenant Governor of the State of Colorado
Candidate for Governor, 1998

"....Entertains, educates, and thoroughly absorbs the reader of any age, offering a unique glimpse into the lives and contributions of women who have had a profound impact on all facets of life in Colorado. ....a gold mine of useful and inspirational information. ....Superb writing and illustrations by Vivian Sheldon Epstein."

Sherman G. Finesilver, Retired Chief Judge
United States District Court for the District of Colorado

"Women have made so many outstanding contributions to this great country of ours. It's wonderful to finally see a well-researched piece of work about the important roles that women played in the history of Colorado. What a refreshing resource for our young people!"

Elizabeth Stansberry, Social Studies Coordinator
Denver Public Schools

"These incredible Colorado women are intriguing! They inspire greater achievements from girls and women who read about them. Vivian Sheldon Epstein has provided a well-researched chronology of the past which has the potential to influence the future."

Nola Wellman, Ph.D., Executive Director of Middle Schools
Cherry Creek School District, Englewood, Colorado

"It is very hard to find much of this information, let alone in one place. Vivian Sheldon Epstein's hours of research have paid off. She has followed her passion, making her a great example for girls."

Keller Hayes, President
Colorado Women's Chamber of Commerce

$16.95